T

Dyslexia
Dictionary

2ND EDITION

British English

Edited by OL COOPER

Dyslexia Dictionary Publishing

1st Edition Published 2020
2nd Edition Published 2024

ISBN 978-1-0686324-2-6

How to Use This Word Finder

The way it works is simple: look up the word as you think it is spelt. If it is correct it will look something like this:

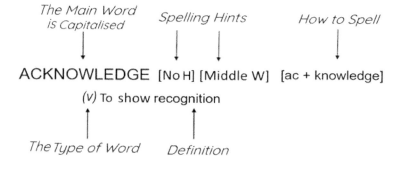

If it is wrong, it will look something like this:

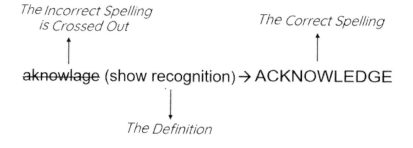

Remember, correct words are always in CAPITALS while ~~incorrect words will be crossed out~~.

Key

Key	Meaning
(adj)	Adjective
(ad)	Adverb
(cap)	Always starts with a capital letter
(con)	Conjunction
Def :	Definition
(folklore)	From stories and likely does not exist
(interjection)	Used to express a feeling
(n)	Noun
(old)	Outdated and/ or rarely used
(pl)	Plural
(prep)	Preposition
(pro)	Pronoun
(v)	Verb

A

Aa

AARDVARK [Three A's] [Hidden D]
[AA-RD-VARK]

(n) A long snouted mammal from Africa

Ab

ABATE [A-BATE]

(v) To become less intense or widespread

ABBREVIATE [Double B] [AB-BRE-VI-ATE]

(v) To shorten a word or phrase

ABDUCT [AB-DUCT]

(v) To take someone against their will;
To kidnap

~~abjective~~ (describing word) → ADJECTIVE
(See 'Sentence Construction')

~~abjective~~ (goal) → OBJECTIVE

ABSCESS [Hidden -SC-] [AB-SC-ESS]

(n) Swelling;
A boil

Ac

~~acurate~~ (precise) → ACCURATE

---

*Be aware of ACC words as the
sound may be hidden.*

Here are some, but not all, examples:

ACCEPT *(v)*

ACCESS *(n)*

ACCIDENT *(n)*

ACCIDENTALLY *(n)* [Single T]

ACCLAIM *(v)*

ACCLIMATISE *(v)*

Acclimatize is US English only

ACCOMPLISH *(v)*

ACCOUNTABLE *(adj)*

ACCUMULATE *(v)* [Double C] [One M]

ACCURATE [Double C]

(adj) To do something without errors

ACCURACY *(n)*

ACCURATELY *(adj)*

ACKNOWLEDGE [AC-KNOWLEDGE]

(v) To show recognition

ACQUIRE [AC-QUIRE]

(v) To obtain

ACRE [not acre] [AC-RE]

(n) An old unit of land measurement

Ad

ADAMANT [No E] [AD-A-MANT]

(adj) Refusing to be convinced.

ADDRESS [Double D] [Double S] [ADD-RESS]

(adj) The location of someone or something

~~adgast~~ (shocked) → AGHAST

~~adgitate~~ (provoke) → AGITATE

ADHERE [AD-HERE]

(v) To follow

Ad

~~adiment~~ (convinced) → ADAMANT

~~adiring~~ (follow) → ADHERE

~~adjar~~ (slightly open) → AJAR

ADJOURN [No E] [AD-JOUR-N]

(v) To breakaway until a future date

ADJUDICATE [AD-JUD-I-CATE]

(v) To make a judgement

~~aduct~~ (take) → ABDUCT

ADVANTAGE [AD-VAN-TAGE]

(n) A favourable situation or occurrence

ADVERSE [AD-VERSE]

   (adj) Harmful

 or

AVERSE [A-VERSE]

   (adj) Dislike;
          Repelled

~~advoid~~ (hide) → AVOID

AERATE [No I] [AE-RATE]

(v) To add air

AERIAL [One I] [AE-R-IAL]

Def 1: *(n)* A device that transmits or revives signals

Def 2: *(adj)* Relating to objects in the air

AERODYNAMIC [AERO-DYN-A-MIC]

(n) The science of air flow and objects movement through air

AEROPLANE [No I] [AERO-PLANE]

(n) An engine powered flying vehicle

AEROSOL [No I] [AERO-SOL]

(n) An object that uses pressure to release gases

AESTHETIC [Silent A] [A-E-ST-HETIC]

(n) Beauty

Esthetic is US English only

Af

Be aware of AF words as the second F's sound may be hidden:

AFFILIATE [A-FF-ILI-ATE]

AFFIRM [A-FF-IRM]

AFFIX [AF-FIX]

AFFLUENT [A-FF-LU-ENT]

AFFORD [AF-FORD]

AFFRAY [AFF-RAY]

AFFRONT [AF-FRONT]

AFFECT [Double F] [A-FF-ECT]

   (n) Something that WILL make a difference

or

EFFECT [Double F] [E-FF-ECT]

   (n) Something that HAS made a difference

AFFIDAVIT [AFF-I-DAVIT]

   (n) A sworn statement

AGGRESSION [Double G] [Double S] [AGG-RE-SS-ION]

(n) Hostile

AGHAST [Semi-silent H] [A-GH-AST]

(adj) Horrified

AGITATE [A-GI-TATE]

(v) To provoke

Ai

AID [No E] [A-ID]

> *(n)* To help

vs

AIDE [A-ID-E]

> *(n)* An assistant to a leader

Be careful of *AER-* and *AIR-* mix-ups:

~~airate~~ (add air) → AERATE

~~aireal~~ (signals) → AERIAL

~~airoplane~~ (aircraft) → AEROPLANE
Airplane is US English only

~~airesol~~ (spray container) → AEROSOL

Aj

AJAR [No D] [A-JAR]

> *(adv) (adj)* Slightly open

~~ajective~~ (describing word) → ADJECTIVE
(See 'Sentence Construction')

~~ajourne~~ (delay) → ADJOURN

~~aknowlage~~ (recognises) → ACKNOWLEDGE

ALIGN [No E] [A-LI-GN]

(v) To ally with;
To place in the correct position

ALLEGE [Double L] [A-LL-EGE]

(v) To make an accusation

ALPHABET [No F] [ALPHA-BET]

(n) The writing of letters as set by a
language

ALREADY [One L] [AL-READY]

(adv) Sooner than expected

ALUMINIUM [AL-U-MIN-IUM]

(n) A metallic element

Chemical element symbol = **AL**
Atomic number = **13**

ALZHEIMER'S DISEASE [No T]
[AL-ZH-E-IM-ER'S DI-SEASE]

(n) A condition that affects the brain and
memory

Am

AMATEUR [Two A's] [AM-A-TEUR]

(n) Not professional

AMBIDEXTROUS [AM-BID-EX-TROUS]

(adj) Able to use both hands with equal ease

AMBITIOUS [AM-BIT-I-OUS]

(adj) Determined to achieve a difficult target

AMEND [Only one M] [A-MEND]

(v) To make changes

AMOK [No C] [A-MOK]

(adv) Out of control

AMUCK is also acceptable

AMPHIBIAN [AMP-HIB-IAN]

(n) Animals that can live both in land and underwater

AMPHITHEATRE [AMPHI-THE-ATRE]

(n) A round structure with seats surrounding a stage

AMPLIFY [AMP-LI-FY]

(v) To make stronger

ANCESTOR [AN-CEST-OR]

(n) A descendant

ANAESTHETIC [AN-AE-ST-HETIC]

(n) A drug or gas that stops pain being felt

ANALOGUE [Ending -UE] [ANA-LOG-UE]

(n) Using physical effects to display
information, as opposed to digitally

ANALYSE [No I] Middle Y] [AN-AL-Y-SE]

(v) To examine

ANGEL [ANG-EL]

(n) A spiritual being;
A good person

or

ANGLE [ANG-LE]

(n) The distance between two lines in
degrees

An

ANEURYSM [AN-EUR-YSM]

(n) A weakness in an artery

~~anisfeckit~~ (pain stopper) → ANAESTHETIC

ANNIVERSARY [Double N] [Ending -SARY]
[ANNI-VER-SARY]

(n) The annual date of an event.

ANONYMOUS [No I] [No E] [ANON-Y-MOS]

(adj) A hidden identity.

ANORAK [Greenlandic] [No ER] [AN-OR-AK]

(n) A waterproof jacket

ANSWER [AN-S-WER]

(n) Respond to

ANTARCTICA [ANT-ARC-TICA]

(n) The Earth's southernmost continent

~~anurisum~~ (blockage) → ANEURYSM

APOLOGY [Single P] [A-POL-OGY]

(n) An expression of regret

APOCALYPSE [Single P] [A-POC-AL-Y-PSE]

(n) The end of the world

APOLOGISE [Single P] [A-POL-OG-ISE]

(v) To express regret

Apologize is US English only

APOSTROPHE [Single P] [A-POST-RO-PH-E]

(n) A punctuation mark (')

APPARENT [Double P] [AP-PAR-ENT]

(adj) Seen clearly;
Appearing so

APPARITION [Double P] [No ER]
[AP-PAR-IT-ION]

(adj) A ghostly appearing figure

APPEAL [Double P] [AP-PEAL]

Def 1: *(v)* To be attractive
To make a request or review;

Def 2: *(n)* Attractiveness

Ap

APPLY [Double P] [APP-LY]

    (n) Request

APPETITE [Double P] [APP-E-TITE]

    (n) Hunger

APPROXIMATE [Double P]
                [APP-ROX-I-MATE]

    Def 1: *(adj)* Close but not exact

    Def 2: *(v)* To be close to

~~appulstary~~ (furniture) → UPHOLSTERY

Aq

~~aquire~~ (gain) → ACQUIRE

~~arain~~ (charge) → ARRAIGN

ARBOUR [AR-BOUR]

(n) A seat surround by trees

or

HARBOUR [HAR-BOUR]

Def 1: *(n)* A place for ships to moor

Def 2: *(v)* To secretly keep

ARCHAEOLOGY [AR-CH-AE-OLOGY]

(n) The study of history through buried objects

ARC [AR-C]

Def 1: *(n)* Part of a curve;
A shape;
A mathematics formula;
The development of a story

Def 2: *(v)* To move with a curving
trajectory
To form an electric arc

or

ARK [AR-K]

(n) (Biblical) The ship built by Noah

Ar

ARCH- [ARCH - + (another word)]

(conjunction) Main

(e.g.: ARCH-ENEMY)

vs

ARCH [AR-CH]

(n) A curved structure on a building

ARCHETYPE [AR-CH-E-TYPE]

(n) A typical example

ARCHIPELAGO [AR-CHI-PE-LA-GO]

(n) A group of islands

ARCHITECTURE [AR-CH-I-TECT-URE]

(n) The design and construction of buildings

ARCHIVE [AR-CH-IVE]

(n) A collection stored for prosperity

ARCTIC [Double C] [ARC-TIC]

(adj) Referencing areas of the North Pole

~~ardvarck~~ (animal) → AARDVARK

ARGUMENT [No E] [ARG-U-MENT]
(n) A disagreement, typically heated

ARGUE *(v)* [with an E]

ARGUMENTATIVE *(adj)* [ARGU-without an E]

~~arkepelego~~ (islands) → ARCHIPELAGO

~~arketype~~ (example) → ARCHETYPE

~~arkive~~ (storage) → ARCHIVE

ARMAGEDDON [ARM-A-GED-DON]
(n) (cap) The biblical end of the world

ARRAIGN [DOUBLE R] [No E] [ARR-A-IGN]
(v) To be charged

ARREARS [Double R] [AR-REAR-S]
(n) (pl) Debt

Ar

ARISTOCRACY [ARIS-TO-CRA-CY]

(n) A system in which small yet privileged
class rules

ARTEFACT [Middle E] [ART-E-FACT]

(n) A manmade object

Artifact is US English only

~~arthentic~~ (real) → AUTHENTIC

~~artunm~~ (Season) → AUTUMN

~~arvarck~~ (animal) → AARDVARK

ASPHYXIATE [No F] [AS-PHY-X-ATE]

(v) To remove oxygen

ASSASSINATE [Double ASS] [ASS-ASS-IN-ATE]

(v) To kill for political or religious reasons

ASSIGN [Double S] [AS-SIGN]

(v) To give value to;
To provide a task or duty to

ASSUME [Double S] [AS-SUME]

(v) To accept without evidence;
To take control

~~astocracy~~ (upper class) → ARISTOCRACY

ASTRONAUT [No -GH] [ASTRO-NAUT]

(n) A person who has been into space

ASYLUM [No I] [AS-Y-LUM]

(n) Protection;
(outdated) A building formally used for
housing those with a mental
illness

Au

AUBERGINE [AUD-IE-NCE]

(n) Purple fruit often mistaken as a vegetable

Known as Eggplant in US English only

AUDIENCE [AUD-IE-NCE]

(n) Spectators

AUSTRALIA [AU-ST-RA-LIA]

(proper noun) A country in the southern
hemisphere;
A continent

AUTHENTIC [No R] [AUTH-EN-TIC]

(adj) Original;
Verified as being real

AUTISM [No O] [AU-TISM]

(n) A neurological condition effecting social
skills

~~austtogracy~~ (upper class) → ARISTOCRACY

AUTUMN [No R] [AU-TU-MN]

(n) The season between summer and winter

AVERSE [A-VERSE]

(adj) Dislike;
Repelled

or

ADVERSE [AD-VERSE]

(adj) Harmful

~~avidavid~~ (statement) → AFFIDAVIT

AVOID [A-VOID]

(v) Keep away from

AWNING [AWN-ING]

(v) A cover for a shelter

~~awtisum~~ (condition) → AUTISM

Ax

AXE [AX-E]

(n) A chopping tool

Ax is US English only

AXLE [Ending -LE]

(n) A rod for turning wheels

B

BABBLE [Double B] [BAB-BLE]

> Def 1: *(n)* Confused talk

> Def 2: *(v)* To talk incoherently

or

BABEL [Single B] [BAB-LE]

> *(n)* A mixture of voices

BAIL [BA-IL]

> *(n)* Money paid to be released

or

BALE [BA-LE]

> *(n)* A bundle of (e.g.: hay)

~~bais~~ (prejudice) → BIAS

Ba

BARE [BA-RE]

>   *(adj)* Not covered or clothed

or

BEAR [BE-AR]

>   *(n)* A large mammal

BAR MITZVAH [BAR MITZ-VAH]

>   *(n)* A Jewish religious ceremony

BATED [BATE-D]

>   *(adj)* With suspense
>
>   *Note: 'with BATED breath', not baited*

BATMAN [BAT-MAN]

>   *(n) (old)* An officers orderly or assistant

BATTERY [Double T] [One A] [BA-TT-ERY]

>   *(n)* A cell that provides electricity;
>   A series of small chicken cages;
>   To touch a person illegally

BEAR [BE-AR]

> *(n)* A large mammal
>
> or

BARE [BA-RE]

> *(adj)* Not covered or clothed

~~beeday~~ (toiletry device) → BIDET

BEFORE [Ending E] [BE-FOR-E]

> Def 1: *(prep)* Previous to
>
> Def 2: *(adv)* Ahead of
>
> Def 3: (con) Sooner than

BEGIN [Single G] [BE-GIN]

> *(v)* To start

BELIEF [BE- LI-EF]

> (n) A feeling;
> Faith

Be

BELIEVE [BE-LI-EVE]

(v) To accept as true

BELLIGERENT [Double L] [Ending -ENT] [BELL-I-GER-ENT]

(adj) Aggressive

BELLWETHER [No A] [BELL-WETHER]

(n) A sheep, person or event that leads the way

BENEFACTOR [No I] [BEN-E-FACTOR]

(n) A person who helps others

BENEFIT [Middle E] [BEN-E-FIT]

Def 1: (n) An advantage

Def 2: (v) To gain an advantage

BENEVOLENT [No A] [No I] [BE-NEV-O-LENT]

(adj) Kind;
Well meaning

~~benifactor~~ (helper) → BENEFACTOR

~~benifit~~ (advantage) → BENEFIT

BENIGN [BE-NIGN]

>*(adj)* Gentle;
>Not harmful

~~berockracy~~ (paperwork) → BUREAUCRACY

BESIEGE [I before E] [BE-SIE-GE]

>*(v)* To surround with an army

~~beyoroh~~ (furniture; organisation) →BUREAU

BIANNUAL [Double N] [BI-ANN-UAL]

(adj) Occurring twice in a year

vs

BIENNIAL [Double N] [BI-ENN-IAL]

(adj) Occurring every other year

BIAS [I before A] [BI-AS]

(n) Being against something

BIASED *(adj)*

BIBLE [No A] BIB-LE]

(n) The Christian and Jewish book of scriptures

BIBLIOGRAPHY [BIB-LIO-GRAPH-Y]

(n) A list of books that have been referred to

BICYCLE [BI-CYCLE]

(n) A two wheeled pedal vehicle

BIDET [Pronounced *bee-day*] [BID-ET]

> *(n)* An object used to wash oneself after using the toilet

---

BIENNIAL [Double N] [BI-ENN-IAL]

> *(adj)* Occurring every other year

vs

BIANNUAL [Double N] [BI-ANN-UAL]

> *(adj)* Occurring twice in a year

BIGOT [One G] [BIG-OT]

> *(n)* Intolerant

BIVOUAC [BI-VOU-AC]

> *(n)* Camping without a tent

BI

BLASÉ [Pronounced *blah*-zay] [BLA-SÉ]

(adj) Unimpressed due to being overdone

BLASPHEME [BLAS-PH-EME]

(v) To insult sacred things

BLATANT [Ending -ANT] [BLA-TANT]

(adj) Open;
Unashamed

BLOC [BLOC]

(n) A group of allies

or

BLOCK [BLOC-K]

Def 1: *(n)* A solid mass;
A group of buildings

Def 2: *(v)* To prevent movement

BLUDGEON [BLU-DG-EON]

(v) To hit with a heavy object

~~boofay~~ (food) → BUFFET

BOOKKEEPING [Three double letters in a row]
[BOOK-KEEP-ING]

(n) Keeping financial records

BORDER [No A] [BORD-ER]

Def 1: *(n)* The point of separation

Def 2: *(v)* To put around the edge

BOURGEOIS [Pronounced *boor-zhwah*]
[BOUR-GE-OIS]

(adj) (n) Regarding one middle class person

BOURGEOISE [Produced *boor-zhwah-zee*]
[BOUR-GE-OI-SE]

(n) Regarding the middle class as a whole

BOUTIQUE [BOUTIQUE]

(n) A small, niche shop

BOY [B-OY]

(n) A male child

vs

BUOY [BU-OY]

(n) A sea float

Br

BRIDAL [BRID-AL]

> (adj) Relating to a bride or newly wed

vs

BRIDLE [BOUTIQUE]

> (n) A harness used to control a horse

BRIGADIER [BRIG-A-DIER]

> (n) An army rank above a colonel and below a major-general

BROCCOLI [Double C] [One I] [BROC-CO-LI]

> (n) A green tree like vegetable

BROCHURE [No S] [One H] [BRO-CHURE]

> (n) A booklet to sell products or services

BRONTOSAURUS [BRONTO-SAURUS]

> (n) A plant eating dinosaur with a long neck

BRUISE [Hidden I] [BRU-I-SE]

> (n) An injury

BRUSQUE [Pronounced bru-usk]

> (adj) Abrupt

BUDDHISM [Double D] [Hidden H]
[BUDD-H-ISM]

(n) A religion and philosophical lifestyle
based on teachings of the Buddha

~~budegon~~ (hit) → BLUDGEON

BUFFET [Pronounced *boo-fay* or *buf-fay*]
[BUF-FET]

(n) A meal in which people help themselves

is spelt the same as:

BUFFET [Pronounced *buff-it*] [BUF-FET]

(v) To hit repeatedly

BUOY [BU-OY]

(n) A sea float

vs

BOY [B-OY]

(n) A male child

Bu

BUREAU [Pronounced *byor-oh*] [BUR-EA-U]

(*n*) A writing desk
An organisation

BUREAUCRACY [BUREAU-CR-ACY]

(*n*) Administration

BUSINESS [BUS-IN-ESS]

(*n*) Commercial

By

~~byas~~ (against) → BIAS

~~byclycle~~ (to ride) → BICYCLE

~~byouroh~~ (furniture; organisation) →BUREAU

~~byrockracy~~ (paperwork) → BUREAUCRACY

BYTE [B-YTE]

(*n*) Computer information equal to 8 bits

C

Be aware of K words as they may sound like they start with C.

Here are some, but not all, examples:

~~caleidoscope~~ (colours) → KALEIDOSCOPE

~~cangaroo~~ (animal) → KANGAROO

~~caraoke~~ (singing) → KARAOKE

~~carma~~ (justice) → KARMA

~~catchup~~ (sauce) → KETCHUP

~~cayak~~ (boat) → KAYAK

~~cerfuffle~~ (fuss) → KERFUFFLE

~~cerosene~~ (fuel) → KEROSENE

~~citchin~~ (cooking) → KITCHEN

~~citten~~ (cat) → KITTEN

~~coala~~ (animal) → KOALA

Ca

CABLE [CAB-LE]

> *(n)* A rope made or wire for carrying electric signals

CACHE [French] [Pronounced *cash-e*]

> *(n)* Hidden

CAESAREAN [CAE-SAE-EAN]

> *(n)* A method of childbirth

Cesarean is US English only

~~caleidoscope~~ (colours) → KALEIDOSCOPE

CALF [CA-LF]

> (n) A young animal (i.e. a newborn cow); A muscle on a leg

The plural is CALVES

CALIBRE [Ending -RE] [CAL-I-BRE]

> *(n)* The dimensions of a weapon barrel; The ability of a person

CALVE [CAL-VE]

(v) To give birth to a large animal

~~calve~~ (Leg Muscle) → CALF

unless plural, then it is CALVES

CAMEL [Ending -EL] [CAM-EL]

(n) A humped desert mammal

CAMOUFLAGE [Hidden U] [CAMO-U-FLAGE]

Def 1: *(n)* Disguise to blend in

Def 2: *(v)* To blend in with the environment

CAMPAIGN [Hidden G] [CAM-PA-IGN]

Def 1: *(n)* Organised action to achieve a goal

Def 2: *(v)* To publicly work for a goal

CANDOUR [Hidden U] [CAN-DO-UR]

(n) Open and honest

Candor is US English only

Ca

~~cangaroo~~ (animal) → KANGAROO

CANOE [CAN-OE]

(n) A narrow boat for paddling on water

CAPITALISE [CAP-IT-AL-ISE]

(v) To take advantage of;
To make with a capital letter

CAPITALIZE is also acceptable

CAPACITY [CAP-A-CITY]

(n) Maximum

CAPPUCCINO [Double P] [Double C]
[CAPP-U-CC-INO]

(n) A type of coffee

~~carf~~ (leg) → CALF

CARIBBEAN [One R] [Two B's]
[CAR-I-B-BEAN]

(adj) (cap) Islands in the Caribbean Sea

~~carma~~ (justice) → KARMA

CARNIVORE [CARN-I-VORE]

(n) An animal that only eats meat

CARRIAGE [Double R] [CAR-RIDGE]

(n) A passenger vehicle pulled by animals

~~cashe~~ (hidden) → CACHE

CASTLE [Ending -LE] [CAS-TLE]

(n) A large stone building, typically from the medieval period, fortified against attack

CASUAL [CAS-U-AL]

(adj) Relaxed

CATALOGUE [CAT-A-LOG-UE]

(n) A list of items

Catalog is US English only

~~catapiller~~ (insect) → CATERPILLAR

CATASTROPHE [CAT-A-STRO-PHE]

(n) A disaster

CATASTROPHIC *(adj)*

CATASTROPHICALLY *(adv)*

Ca

CATEGORY [One A] [CAT-E-GORY]

(n) Grouped based on common
characteristics

CATER [Ending -ER] [CAT-ER]

(v) To provide

CATERPILLAR [CAT-ER-PILL-AR]

(n) The larva of a butterfly or moth

CAULIFLOWER [CAULI- FLOWER]

(n) A white-headed vegetable

CAVALRY [CAV-AL-RY]

(n) Soldiers who fought on horseback;
Modern soldiers who use armoured
vehicles

CAVEAT [CAV-E-AT]

(n) An attached warning

~~cayak~~ (boat) → KAYAK

~~cease~~ (take) → SEIZE

~~ceason~~ (part of the year) → SEASON

CELEBRATE [CEL-E-BRATE]

(v) To joyfully acknowledge a special occasion

CELSIUS [CEL-SI-US]

(n) A scale of temperature

~~cense~~ (feeling) → SENSE

CENSOR [CEN-SOR]

Def 1: *(v)* To ban or remove

Def 2: *(n)* A person who removes content prevent others from seeing it

or

CENSURE [CEN-SURE]

(v) To strongly criticize

CENTRE [Ending -RE] [CENT-RE]

(n) The middle

Center is US English only

Ce

CENTIMETRE [Ending -RE] [CENTI-MET-RE]

(n) A hundredth of a metre, or 10 millimetres

> *The shortened form is **cm***

Centimeter is US English only

CEREAL [CE-REAL]

(n) A grain used for food
A food eaten at breakfast

vs

SERIAL [SE-RIAL]

Def 1: *(adj)* Repeating
Taking part in a series

Def 2: *(n)* Media that occurs over
multiple slots

CEREMONIAL [CER-E-MONIAL]

(adj) A religious or public event

~~cerfew~~ (time limit) → CURFEW

~~cerfuffle~~ (fuss) → KERFUFFLE

~~cerinade~~ (to woo) → SERENADE

~~cermon~~ (preach) → SERMON

~~cerosene~~ (fuel) → KEROSENE

~~cernal~~ (rank) → COLONEL

CERTAIN [Hidden I] [CER-TAIN]

> (adj) To be accurate;
> Specific but not explicitly named or stated

~~certan~~ (window covering) → CURTAIN

CESSPOOL [Starting CESS-] [CESS-POOL]

(n) An underground tank for sewage

Also known as a CESSPIT

Ch

CHANDELIER [CHAN-DE-LEIR]

(n) A hanging light

CHAPLAIN [CHAP-LAIN]

(n) A member of the clergy

CHARACTER [Hidden H] [CHARA-CTER]

(n) A person in a story;
The qualities of person

CHARACTERISTICS [CHARACTER-IS-TICS]

Def 1: *(n)* A trait that makes something
different

Def 2: *(adj)* A typical trait

CHARISMA [CHA-RIS-MA]

(n) Inspirational charm

CHATEAU [French] [CHAT-EAU]

(n) A large French house or castle

The plural is CHATEAUX

~~chore~~ (sea) → SHORE

CHAUFFEUR [CHAU-FF-ER]

(n) An employed driver

CHEQUE *[CHE-QU-E[*

(n) A written order to pay funds

Check in a monetary sense is US English only

CHEQUERED [CHE-QU-ER-ED]

(adj) Alternating squares of different
colours;
Varying fortunes

Checkered is US English only

CHIVALROUS [CHIV-AL-ROUS]

(adj) Polite towards women

CHIVALRY [CHIV-AL-RY]

(n) A code on honour among knights

Ch

CHLOROPHYLL [CH-LORO-PHYLL]

(n) A green pigment that plants use convert sunlight to food during photosynthesis

---

CHOOSE [Double O] [CH-OOSE]

(v) To pick

vs

CHOSE [Single O] [CH-OSE]

(v) The past tense of CHOOSE

CINNAMON [Double N] [CINN-A-MON]

(n) A spice

CIPHER [CI-PH-ER]

(n) A code

CYPHER is also acceptable

vs

SIPHON [No F] [SI-PHON]

Def 1: *(n)* A tube used to move liquid via gravity

Def 2: *(v)* To take

~~ciry~~ (question) → QUERY

~~cist~~ (body) → CYST

~~citchin~~ (cooking) → KITCHEN

CITIZEN [No S] [CIT-I-ZEN]

(n) A legally recognised member of a country

~~citten~~ (cat) → KITTEN

~~clawofill~~ (plants) → CHLOROPHYLL

Co

~~coala~~ (animal) → KOALA

COCCYX [COC-CYX]

(n) The bone at the base of the spine

COFFEE [Double E] [CO-FF-EE]

(n) A hot drink made from roasted and ground coffee beans

COINCIDENCE [Double E] [CO-FF-EE]

(n) A chance occurrence without any apparent causal connection

COLONEL [Pronounced *col-nal*] [COL-O-NEL]

(n) An Army rank

COLOUR [COL-OUR]

(n) Appearance

Color is US English only

COLOURFUL [Not -full] [COL-OUR-FUL]

(adj) Having an attractive colour(s); Lively

COMB [No E] [COM-B]

Def 1: *(n)* A device used to tidy hair
Def 2: *(v)* To brush through hair;
To search

or

COMBE [With an E] [COM-BE]

(n) A short valley

COMBAT [No E] [COM-BAT]

(n) Fight

COMMA [No ER] [COM-MA]

(n) A punctuation mark (,)

COMMANDEER [Not -mon] [COM-MAN-DEER]

(v) To officially take possession or control of

COMPARATIVE [COM-PARA-TIVE]

(n) By comparison

COMPETITION [COM-PE-TIT-ION]

(n) An activity to win

Co

CONJURE [CON-JURE]

(n) Appear by magic;
To make someone think

CONSCIENCE [CON-SCIENCE]

(n) A persons morales

CONKER [CON-KER]

(n) A horse chestnut seed

vs

CONQUER

(v) To overcome and control

CONSCIOUS [CON-SCI-OUS]

(adj) Awake;
Deliberate;
Aware

CONSOLE [Not soul] [CON-SOLE]

Def 1: *(n)* A panel on a machine

Def 2: *(v)* To comfort

CONSONANT [No middle T] [CON-SON-ANT]

(n) A type of letter, along with a vowel (e.g.: B, C, D, etc…)

CONSUMMATE [Double M] [CON-SUM-MATE]

(v) To complete a marriage by having sexual intercourse

~~coo~~ (taking power) → COUP

~~corgette~~ (vegetable) → COURGETTE

~~cornel~~ (rank) → COLONEL

CORPORAL [No E] [COR-POR-AL]

Def 1: *(n)* A non-commissioned officer (NCO) rank

Def 2: *(adj)* Regarding the human anatomy

CORPORAL PUNISHMENT

(n) To physically punish

CORRIDOR [Double R] [One ending O] [CO-RR-I-DOR]

(n) A passageway or strip of land linking two areas

Co

COUGAR [COU-GAR]

(n) US name for a Puma, a large feline

Also known as a mountain lion

COUNTRY [COUNT-RY]

(n) A nation

vs

COUNTY [COUN-TY]

(n) Administrative areas of a country

COUP [SILENT P]

(n) Suddenly seizing power;
A successful move

COUPE [COU-PE]

(n) A type of car

COURGETTE [COUR-GET-TE]

(n) A long vegetable with a dark green skin

Known as a Zucchini in US English only

~~cowinidence~~ (luck) → COINCIDENCE

~~coxicx~~ (bone) → COCCYX

CRUISE [I before the U] [CR-U-ISE]

(v) To travel slowly;
   To vacation on a ship

CUE [CUE]

Def 1: *(n)* A signal;
      A long rod for playing pool, snooker or
      billiards

Def 2: *(v)* To signal;
      To line up a shot

~~cue~~ (wait) → QUEUE

CUISINE [Hidden middle I] [CUI-SINE]

(n) A style of cooking

CURFEW [Starting CUR-] CUR-FEW]

(n) A time restriction to stay indoors

CURTAIN [Starting CUR-] [CUR-TAIN]

(n) Cloth that covers windows

CUSTOMER [CUST-O-MER]

(n) A person buying something

Cy

CYMBAL [No E] [CY-M-BAL]

(n) A percussion instrument

CYPHER [CY-PH-ER]

(n) A code; unimportant

CIPHER is also acceptable

CYST [CY-ST]

(n) An abnormal fluid sack/ cavity in the body.

D

Da

DAFFODIL [DAFF-O-DIL]

(n) A type of plant

DAUGHTER [DAU-GHT-ER]

(n) Relation of a girl to their mother or father

~~day ja voo~~ (experience) → DÉJÀ VU

De

DEBRIS [Pronounced *DE-BREE*] [DE-BR-IS]

(n) Broken pieces of a larger object

DECISION [DE-CI-SION]

(n) A choice

DEFEAT [DE-FEAT]

Def 1: *(v)* To beat

Def 2: *(n)* Defeating or being defeated

DEFENCE [DE-FENCE]

(n) To defend;
To justify;
To counter-argue

Defense is US English only

DEFENDANT [Ending -ANT] [DE-FEND-ANT]

(n) The accused

DEFINITE [Ending E] [DEF-IN-ITE]

(adj) Clear;
Certain

DEFUSE [DE-FUSE]

(v) To reduce tension;
   To remove a fuse

or

DIFFUSE [DIF-FUSE]

Def 1: *(n)* Not concentrated in one area

Def 2: *(v)* To spread out;
   To intermingle gases and liquids
   with other substances

DEFY [DE-FY]

(v) Openly resist;
   Challenge

DÉJÀ VU [French] [Pronounced *day-zhah-voo*]

(n) The feeling of having already experienced
   something

~~delexia~~ (leaning condition) → DYSLEXIA

DELICIOUS [DEL-IC-OUS]

(adj) Tasty

De

DENIAL [DE-NIAL]

(n) Refusal to accept something unpleasant

DENY [Ending Y] [DE-NY]

(v) To state that something isn't true;
To prevent

DEOXYRIBONUCLEIC ACID
[DE – OXY – RIB – O – NUCLEIC ACID]

(n) The chemical in the cells of animals and
that carries genetic information
(often shortened to DNA)

DEPOSIT [No ending E] [DE-POS-IT]

Def 1: *(n)* Money used to secure something;
Money in a bank

Def 2: *(v)* To store safely;
To place

~~desater~~ (event) → DISASTER

~~descover~~ (find) → DISCOVER

~~desease~~ (illness) → DISEASE

DESERT [DE-SERT]

>   Def 1: *(n)* A waterless environment

>   Def 2: *(v)* To abandon

or

DESSERT [DE-SS-ERT]

>   *(n)* A sweet course at the end of a meal

~~descise~~ (change appearance) → DISGUISE

~~desel~~ (fuel) → DIESEL

DESPITE [DE-SPITE]
(prep) Not being affected by

~~desision~~ (choice) → DECISION

~~deskyse~~ (change appearance) → DISGUISE

De

~~deva~~ (difficult to please person) → DIVA

DEVELOP [No ending E] [DE-VEL-OP]

> *(v)* To make larger and/or more advanced;
> To start;
> To convert land for a new purpose;
> To treat a film to generate images

Be careful of DIV- words:

~~devine~~ (holy) → DIVINE

~~devisable~~ (dividable) → DIVISIBLE

~~devision~~ (separate) → DIVISION

~~devisive~~ (disagreement) → DIVISIVE

~~diafram~~ (muscle) → DIAPHRAGM

DIAGNOSIS [DI-AGN-OSIS]

(n) Identification of an illness or problem

DIAMOND [Hidden A] [DI-A-MOND]

(n) A precious stone;
A 4-sided shape

DIAPHRAGM [No F] [DIA-PH-RA-G-M]

(n) The layer of muscle between the lungs
and the stomach;
A contraceptive cap

DIARRHOEA [DI-A-RR-HO-EA]

(n) A condition of passing liquid faeces

Diarrhea is US English only

DICTIONARY [DIC-TION-ARY]

(n) A book or digital resource containing
information about words

~~didital~~ (information) → DIGITAL

Di

DIE [D-IE]

Def 1:*(v)* To stop living

Def 2: *(n)* The singular of dice; a cast

or

DYE [D-YE]

Def 1: *(n)* A product used to colour
something
Def 2: *(v)* To colour something with dye

~~diegest~~ (process food) → DIGEST

DIESEL [DIE-SEL]

(n) A fuel;
A type of engine

DIET [DIE-T]

Def 1: *(n)* What something consumes

Def 2: *(v)* To restrict food to lose weight

Careful of the double F:

DIFFER [DIF-FER] *(v)*

DIFFERENCE [DIFF-ER-ENCE] *(n)*

DIFFERENT [DIFF-ER-ENT] *(adj)*

DIFFICULT [DIFF-I-CULT] *(adj)*

DIFFICULTY [DIFF-I-CULT-Y] *(n)*

DIFFRACT [DIFF-RACT] *(v)*

DIFFUSE [DIF-FUSE]

Def 1: *(n)* Not concentrated in one area;
Unclear

Def 2: *(v)* To spread out;
To intermingle gases and liquids
with other substances

or

DEFUSE [DE-FUSE]

(v) To reduce tension;
To remove a fuse

Di

DIGITAL [DIG-ITAL]

(n) Information existing in code

DIGNIFY [DIG-NI-FY]

(n) Worthy of respect

DINOSAUR [DINO-SAUR]

(n) Extinct, prehistoric animals

DISASTER [DIS-A-STER]

(n) A sudden event that causes damages;
A sudden misfortune

DISASTROUS [DIS-AS-TROUS]

(n) Causing great damage;
Going wrong

DISC [DI-SC]

(n) A flat, circular object;
A data storage device;
A layer of cartilage in the spine

Disk is US English only

DISCIPLINE [DIS-CIP-LINE]

Def 1: *(n)* Obedience

Def 2: *(v)* To train;
To punish

~~discise~~ (change appearance) → DISGUISE

DISCOVER [DIS-COVER]

(v) To find;
To gain knowledge of

> ## DISCREET [Double E] [DIS-CREET]
>
> *(adj)* Careful to keep something hidden
>
> *or*
>
> ## DISCRETE [DIS-CRETE]
>
> *(n) An* independent existence

DISEASE [DIS-EASE]

(n) An illness

DISGUISE [DIS-GU-ISE]

Def 1: *(n)* Altering an appearance to hide an
identity

Def 2: *(v)* To alter an appearance to hide an
identity

Di

DISHONOUR [DIS-HON-OUR]

Def 1: *(n)* Shame

Def 2: *(v)* To bring shame;
To fail to keep an agreement

Dishonor is US English only

DISINTERESTED [DIS-INTER-EST-ED]

(adj) Not biased

or

UNINTERESTED [UN-INTER-EST-ED]

(adj) Not caring

~~dislexia~~ (leaning condition) → DYSLEXIA

DISOBEY [DIS-OBEY]

(v) To fail to follow orders or directions

~~dispite~~ (in spite of) → DESPITE

DISTIL [DIS-TIL]

(v) To purify a liquid;
   To get the most important aspects

Distill is US English only

DIVA [Pronounced *dee-va*] [DI-VA]

(n) A difficult to please person

DIVINE [DI-VINE]

Def 1: *(adj)* Regarding to a God or a god like
   figure

Def 2: *(v)* Discover by instinct

DIVISIBLE [DI-VIS-IBLE]

(adj) Capable of being divided or shared

DIVISION [DI-VISION]

Def 1: *(n)* The sum of the parts

Def 2: *(v)* To divide;
   To partition

DIVISIVE [DI-VIS-IVE]

(adj) Cause disagreement

Dn

DNA = DEOXYRIBONUCLEIC ACID
[DE – OXY – RIB – O – NUCLEIC ACID]

(n) The chemical in the cells of animals and that carries genetic information

Do

DOES [DO-ES]

[3 RD PERSON] Present tense of DO

or

DOSE [DO-SE]

(n) Quantity (e.g.: radiation or medicine)

DOUGHNUT [DOUGH-NUT]

(n) Fried dough in the shape of a ball or ring

DONUT is also acceptable but is seen as US English

~~doorter~~ (child) → DAUGHTER

DOUBT [DO-U-BT]

Def 1: *(n)* A lack of trust

Def 2: *(v)* To question if something is truthful

DRAFT [DRA-FT]

Def 1: *(n)* Not the final version;
A written order to a bank

Def 2: *(v)* To prepare a draft;
To select someone

sounds the same as

DRAUGHT [DR-AU-GHT]

Def 1: *(n)* A current cool air in a room;
A board game (*chequers*)

Def 2: *(adj)* From a cask;
An animal using for pulling

Draft in these contexts is US English

DWARF [D-WARF]

Def 1: *(n)* A short, hardy mythical being in
folklore and fantasy

Def 2: *(v)* To make something seem small

Def 3: *(adj)* Denoting a smaller species,
usually of a plant or animal

DYE [D-YE]

Def 1: *(n)* A product used to colour
    something

Def 2: *(v)* To colour something with dye

or

DIE [D-IE]

Def 1: *(v)* To stop living

Def 2: *(n)* The singular of dice;
    A cast

DYSLEXIA [DYS-LEX-IA]

(n) A common learning difficulty that mainly
    causes problems with reading, writing and
    spelling

DYSLEXIC *(adj) (n)*

~~dyuhfram~~ (muscle) → DIAPHRAGM

E

EAGER [EA-G-ER]

(adj) Wanting to do or have something

EAGLE [Hidden A] [E-A-G-L-E]

(n) A bird of prey

EASE [E-A-SE]

Def 1: *(n)* easy; relaxed

Def 2: *(v)* To remove tension;
To move gently

EASEL [EASE-L]

(n) A support artists use to for painting

EASY [Ending Y] [EA-SY]

(adj) Achieved simply;
Worry free

EAVES [EA-VES]

(pl) (n) The overhanging edges of a roof

EAVESDROP [EA-VES-DROP]

(v) To listen without permission

Eb

ebate (reduce) → ABATE

Ec

ECHELON [E-CHE-LON]

(n) A level within an organisation or profession.

ECONOMY [No A] [ECO-NO-MY]

(n) The process or system by which goods and services are produced, sold and consumed within a country or region; Cheaper version(s)

ecpose (report) → EXPOSÉ

ECSTASY [Hidden S] [Ending -SY] [EC-S-TA-SY]

(n) Extreme happiness;
(cap) An illegal drug

EDGE [ED-GE]

Def 1: *(n)* Outside of an object;
An advantage;
The sharpened side of a blade

Def 2: *(v)* To provide with an advantage;
To move closer

Ee

EEL [Double E] [EEL]

(n) A snake-like fish.

~~eeri~~ (an eagle's nest) → EYRIE

EERIE [Double E] [EE-R-IE]

(adj) Scary

Ef

EFFECT [Double F] [E-FF-ECT]

> *(n)* Something that HAS made a difference

or

AFFECT [Double F] [A-FF-ECT]

> *(n)* Something that WILL make a difference

Eg

~~ege~~ (side) → EDGE

~~eght~~ (number) → EIGHT

EGYPT [E-GY-PT]

(proper noun) An African country

Eh

~~ehpuhlet~~ (uniform) → EPAULETTE

EIGHT [Hidden I] [E-I-GHT]

>   *(adj) (n)* The number 8

EIGHTY [Hidden I] [E-I-GHT-Y]

>   *(adj) (n)* The number 80

~~ekual~~ (same standing) → EQUAL

ELEPHANT [EL-E-PHANT]

>   *(n)* A very large grey mammal with a trunk

ELICIT [EL-LICT]

>   *(v)* To draw a reaction

vs

ILLICIT [IL-LI-CIT]

>   *(adj)* Unlawful;
>   Rude

Em

Be careful that the word is EM-, not IM or EN:

EMBANKMENT [EM-BANK-MENT]

(n) Raised earth

EMBARGO [EM-BAR-GO]

Def 1: *(n)* A trade ban with another country

Def 2: *(v)* To ban

EMBARK [EM-BARK]

(v) To start;
To enter an aeroplane or ship

EMBARRASS [Double R, Double S]
[EM-BAR-RASS]

(v) To cause self-consciousness or shame

EMBODY [EM-BODY]

(v) To give a physical form to an ideal;
To contain

EMBRYO [EM-BR-YO]

(n) Unborn or unhatched offspring (in humans this is classified as pre-eight weeks development, after which it becomes classified as a FETUS)

EMPHASIZE [Hidden H] [EM-PHA-SIZE]

(v) To draw special attention to

EMPEROR [EMP-ER-OR]

(n) A male ruler

EMPRESS [EMP-RESS]

(n) A female ruler

vs

IMPRESS [MP-RESS]

(v) To make someone feel admiration; To push a design or mark in

En

ENCLAVE [EN-CLAVE]

(n) A piece of territory surrounded by a larger,
socially different territory

ENCLOSE [EN-CLOSE]

(n) To contain;
To give

ENCOMPASS [EM-COMP-ASS]

(v) To encircle
To include

ENCOURAGE [EN-COURAGE]

(v) To support

ENCROACH [EN-CRO-ACH]

(v) To intrude

ENCRYPT [EN-CRY-PT]

(v) To hide behind code

ENCUMBER [EN-CUM-BER]

(v) To imped

ENTHUSIASM [EN-TH-US-IA-SM]

(n) Great interest and approval

En

ENCORE [EN-CORE]

> Def 1: *(n)* An extra performance at the end

> Def 2: *(n)* To call for an extra performance

ENDEAVOUR [Hidden A] [EN-DEAV-OUR]

> Def 1: *(v)* To try

> Def 2: *(n)* A determined effort

ENGINEER [Double ending E] [EN-GIN-EER]

> Def 1: *(v)* To design;
>   To organise

> Def 2: *(n)* A person who maintains
>   machinery

ENTIRE [EN-TIRE]

> *(adj)* The whole;
>   Nothing left out

ENTIRELY [EN-TIRE-LY]

> *(adv)* The whole;
>   Nothing left out

ENTIRETY [EN-TIRE-TY]

> *(n)* The whole

En

ENTREPRENEUR [ENTRE-PRE-NEUR]

(n) A person who creates businesses

ENTHUSIASM

(n) Great interest or approval

ENVELOPE [EN-VE-LOPE]

(n) For sending out letters

ENVIRONMENT [Hidden N]
[EN-VIRO-N- MENT]

(n) The surroundings or conditions in which a person, animal, or plant lives or operates

ENZYME [EN-ZY-ME]

(n) Proteins that help speed up the chemical reactions in our bodies.

Eo

EON [E-ON]

(n) An undefined, long period of time

EPAULETTE [French] [E-PAUL-ETTE]

(n) Shoulder pieces on a uniform

EPONYMOUS [E-PONY-MOUS]

(adj) Named after something or someone

~~epostraphe~~ (') → APOSTROPHE

EQUAL [E-QU-AL]

Def 1: *(adj)* The same qualities;
      (adj) Even

Def 2: *(v)* To match something

Def 3: *(n)* A person or thing that is the same in status or quality

EQUALISE [E-QU-AL-ISE]

(v) To make equal

EQUALIZE is also acceptable

EQUINE [E-QU-INE]

(adj) Related to horses;
      Regarding the animal family Equidae, which comprises of horses, zebras, and asses

Er

erraign (bring forward) → ARRAIGN

Es

ese (relaxed) → EASE
or
ese (simple) → EASY

esfixiate (strangle) → ASPHYXIATE

eshulon (level) → ECHELON

esophagus (body part) → OESOPHAGUS
(US English)

estrogen (hormone) → OESTROGEN
(US English)

esthetic (Style) → AESTHETIC
(US English)

~~ether~~ (choice) → EITHER

ETIQUETTE [HIDDEN -QU-] [ETI-QU-ETTE]

(n) The unwritten rules of society

EUCALYPTUS [Starting with an E] [E-UCAL-YP-TUS]

(n) An Australian tree that is used to make essential oils, favoured by Koalas

Ev

EVIDENCE [Starting EVI-] [EVI-DEN-CE]

(n) The available facts and information that indicate and support an answer

EVIDENCED [Starting EVI-] [EVI-DEN-CED]

(v) To provide or be proof of

EVIDENTLY [Starting EVI-] [EVI-DEN-TLY]

(adv) Clearly seen;
It would seem that

Ex

EXACERBATE [No S] [EX-ACER-BATE]

(v) To make something worse

vs

EXASPERATE [EX-A-SPER-ATE]

(v) To irritate

EXAMINE [Ending E] [EX-AM-IN-E]

(v) To check closely;
To test

EXERCISE [No C] [EX-ER-CISE]

Def 1: *(n)* Physical activity
A task that tests or practice a skill.

Def 2: *(v)* To do physical activity;
The use of power;
To test or practice a skill.

EXHIBIT [EX-HIB-IT]

Def 1: *(v)* To display in public;
To display a quality

Def 2: *(n)* An object on public display

EXHIBITION *(n)*

EXPERIENCE [No A] [EX-PER-I-EN-CE]

Def 1: *(n)* Involvement;
Knowledge or skills acquired

Def 2: *(v)* To be affected by

EXPOSÉ [EX-PO-SÉ]

(n) A media report which reveals the truth about a situation or person

EXTINCT [EX-TIN-CT]

(adj) (of a living being) Having no living members;
(of a volcano) No longer erupting

EXTREME [EX-TR-EME]

Def 1: *(adj)* The highest degree;
Unusual;
The furthest point from something

Def 2: *(n)* The furthest point between two things

EXTINGUISH [EX-TIN-GU-ISH]

(v) To end

Ey

EYRIE [E-Y-RIE]

(n) An eagles nest

F

Fa

FABRICATE [FAB-RI-CATE]

(v) To create a lie;
To make

FAECES [Hidden A] F-A-ECES]

(n) Bodily waste

Feces is US English only

FALLACY [No E] [FALL-A-CY]

(n) A mistaken belief;
Poor reasoning

~~fallas~~ (penis) → PHALLUS

FALSIFY [No U] [FAL-SI-FY]

(v) To alter something to be incorrect

FAMILIAL [FAM-ILI-AL]

(adj) Relating to family

Fa

FAMILIAR [FAM-ILI-AR]

Def 1: *(adj)* Well known;
Having knowledge of;
Comfortable

Def 2: *(n)* (In folklore) A spirit attached to a witch

FAMILIARISE [FAM-ILI-A-RISE]

(v) To get knowledge of;
To get comfortable with

Also acceptable is FAMILIARIZE

FAMOUS [No E] [FAM-OUS]

(adj) Widley known

~~faness~~ (precision) → FINESSE

FANTASISE [FAN-TA-SISE]

(v) To imagine in a desirable way

Fantasize is US English only

FANTASY [FAN-TA-SY]

(n) Fiction;
Unrealistic Dreams;
Happy scenarios

~~fantom~~ (ghost) → PHANTOM

~~fairo~~ (Egyptian ruler) → PHARAOH

~~farage~~ (search) → FORAGE

FARTHER [FAR-THER]

      (adv) Distant with a physical measurement
            available

or

FATHER [FA-THER]

     Def 1: *(n)* A male parent;
            Founder;
            Priest

     Def 2: *(v)* (Male only) To create

or

FURTHER [FUR- THER]

     Def 1: *(adv)* Distant (unknown distance);

     Def 2: *(adj)* Additional;
             More Distant

     Def 3: *(n)* To help promote

Fa

FASCINATE [Hidden C] [FAS-CIN-ATE]

(v) To interest

FASCISM [Hidden C] [FAS-C-ISM]

(n) Extreme, right wing political views

~~fase~~ (gradual; staged) → PHASE

or

~~fase~~ (surprise) → FAZE

FATHER [FA-THER]

Def 1: *(n)* A male parent;
Founder;
A priest

Def 2: *(v)* (Male only) To create

FATIGUE [FAT-I-GUE]

Def 1: *(n)* Tiredness;
Weakness in metal;
Expendable military clothing

Def 2: *(v)* To make tired

FAUX PAS [Pronounced *foh-pah*] [FA-UX PAS]

(n) A social error

~~faw~~ (defrost) → THAW

FAWN [FA-WN]

Def 1: *(n)* A baby deer;
A light brown colour

Def 2: *(v)* To please by being overly affectionate

FAZE [FA-ZE]

(v) To shock

FEBRUARY [Hidden R] [FEB-R-U-ARY]

(n) The second month of the year

~~feces~~ (bodily waste) → FAECES

FEDERAL [Not -real] [FED-ER-AL]

(adj) A system of government in which individual areas or states have control over their own affairs but are under the control of a central government

FEMUR [No A] [FE-MUR]

(n) The upper leg bone

Also known as the thigh bone

Fe

feenix (mythological bird) → PHOENIX

feme (subject) → THEME

fenominal (fantastic) → PHENOMENAL

feord (body of water) → FJORD or FIORD

ferimone (scent) → PHEROMONE

ferory (explanation) → THEORY

FERTILE [FER-TILE]

(adj) Producing crops or vegetation;
Producing offspring;
Productive

FERTILISE [FERT-IL-ISE]

(v) To introduce sperm; to introduce pollen;
To mix into soil to make something more
productive

FETUS [FE-TUS]

(n) Unborn offspring (in humans this is
classified as eight weeks or more
development, before which it is classified
as an EMBRYO)

FOETUS is also acceptable

FIANCÉ [French] [FI-AN-CÉ]

(n) The MALE you are due to marry

vs

FIANCÉE [French] [Double E] [FI-AN-C-ÉE]

(n) The FEMALE you are due to marry

FIANCHETTO [Italian] [FIAN-CHET-TO]

Def 1: (n) In chess, the early development of a
bishop towards the edge of the board

Def 2: (v) To move fianchetto

FIBRE [Ending in -RE] [FIB-RE]

(n) A strand of thread used to make textiles;
A dietary material that is difficult to digest

FINALE [Pronounced *fin-ah-lee*] [FIN-AL-E]

(n) The final part

FINESSE [FIN-ESS-E]

(n) Precision handling

FINITE [FI-NITE]

(adj) Limited

FJORD [F-J-ORD]

> *(n)* A long, deep narrow body of water with steep slopes

Also acceptable is FIORD

FLAUNT [FL-AUNT]

> *(v)* To proudly display

or

FLOUT [FL-OUT]

> *(v)* To openly disregard rules

~~flem~~ (mucus) → PHLEGM

~~flegmatic~~ (calm) → PHLEGMATIC

~~foh pas~~ (social error) → FAUX PAS

~~fokelore~~ (story) → FOLKLORE

FOLIAGE [Not FOIL-] [FOL-I- AGE]

(n) Leaves

FOLKLORE [FOLK-LORE]

(n) Traditional stories of a community that are passed through the generations by word of mouth

~~fonectic~~ (sounds) → PHONETIC

FORAGE [FOR-AGE]

(v) To search nature for food and supplies

FOREIGN [FOR-E-IGN]

(adj) From another country; from outside

FORTUNE [FORT-UNE]

(n) Chance or luck;
A vast amount of money

Fr

FRIEND [I before END] [FR-I-END]

Def 1: *(n)* A person or animal that you
personally know and find
agreeable;
A supporter

Def 2: *(v)* To connect with online

FRIVOLOUS [FRI-VO-LOUS]

(adj) Not necessary to an unusual degree;
Not being treated as serious

~~fulseify~~ (edit) → FALSIFY

FUNDAMENTAL [Hidden A]
[FUND-A-MENTAL]

Def 1: *(adj)* Of necessary importance

Def 2: *(n)* A Basic rule

FURTHER [FUR- THER]

Def 1: *(adv)* Distant (unknown distance)

Def 2: *(adj)* Additional;
More Distant

Def 3: *(v)* To help promote
or

FARTHER [FAR-THER]

(adv) Distant with a physical measurement available

FURLOUGH [FUR-LOUGH]

(n) An approved period of absence

FURNITURE [FURN-I-TURE]

(n) Moveable items in a building

~~furtile~~ (producing) → FERTILE

Fu

FUTURE [One R] [FU-TURE]

> Def 1: *(n)* Still to occur at a later time;
> Assets brought at a set price but
> are delivered later

> Def 2: *(adj)* Going to occur at a late time

Fy

~~fynight~~ (limited) → FINITE

~~fyord~~ (body of water) → FJORD or FIORD

G

Ga

GAELIC [GA-E-LIC]

(cap) (n) A Celtic language spoken in Ireland and Scotland

GAFF [GA-FF]

(n) A hooked stick used for fishing

or

GAFFE [GA-FF-E]

(n) A blunder

GAIT [GA-IT]

(n) The way someone or something walks

vs

GATE [GA-TE]

(n) A hinged entrance on an opening

Ga

GANGRENE [Not -green] [GAN-GRENE]

(n) The localised death of bodily tissue

GAUGE [GA-U-GE]

Def 1: *(n)* A measuring instrument;
The distance in between railway tracks

Def 2: *(v)* To guess measurements

Gage is US English only

~~gaylic~~ (language) → GAELIC

Ge

GENUINE [GEN-U-INE]

(adj) Honest;
As stated;
Real

~~geraffe~~ (animal) → GIRAFFE

Gh

GHASTLY [GH-AST-LY]

(adj) Gruesome;
Dreadful;
Resembling a ghost

GHOST [GH-OST]

(n) An apparition of a dead person or animal

GHOUL [GH-OUL]

(n) A demonic creature in folklore;
Excessively interested in death

Gi

GIGOLO [GIG-O-LO]

>*(n)* A man paid by a woman to be her lover

~~gihad~~ (war against non-believers) → JIHAD

GILD [GI-LD]

>*(v)* To thinly cover in gold

GILET [Pronounced *zhi-lay*] [GI-LET]

>*(n)* A sleeveless padded jacket

~~gillotine~~ (bladed machine) → GUILLOTINE

GILT [GIL-T]

>Def 1: *(n)* A thin layer of gold

>Def 2: *(adj)* Covered with a thin layer of gold

or

GUILT [GU-ILT]

>*(n)* The feeling of having wronged; Having committed or been found to have committed an offence

---

~~gilt~~ (abandon) → JILT

~~ginx~~ (curse) → JINX

GIRAFFE [Double F] [GIR-AFF-E]

(n) A large, long necked African mammal

GIST [GI-ST]

(n) A general sense of something

GI

GLACÉ [GLA-CÉ]

    (adj) Preserved in sugar

vs

GLAZE [GLA-ZE]

    Def 1: *(n)* A shiny surface

    Def 2: *(v)* To cover with glass;
            To lose brightness

GLAMOUR [GLAM-OUR]

    (n) Attractive qualities that makes things seem appealing

GLAMORIZE [No S] [No U] [GLAMOR-IZE]

    (n) To glorify or romanticise

GLAMOROUS [One U] [GLAM-OR-OUS]

    (adj) Attractive in an exciting way

GLEAM [GLE-AM]

Def 1: *(v)* To shine via reflected light

Def 2: *(n)* Brief sign if quality;
Brief light

or

GLEAN [GLE-AN]

(n) To gather (e.g.: information)

Gn

GNAW [Silent G] [G-NAW]

(v) To bite or nibble at something persistently

GNOME [Silent G] [G-NOME]

(n) (folklore) A tiny human-like being;
A garden ornament

Go

GOES [Starting GO-] [GO-ES]

[3RD Person] Present tense of GO

GORGEOUS [GORGE-OUS]

(adj) Stunning;
Beautiful

~~gost~~ (spirit) → GHOST

Gr

GRAFFITI [Double f] [Single T] [GRAF-FI-TI]

(n) Unwanted writing or artwork in public spaces

GRAMMAR [No E] [GRAM-MAR]

(n) The structure of a language

GRANITE [Ending E] [GRAN-ITE]

(n) A type of very hard rock

GRATEFUL [Not *great*-] [GRATE-FUL]

(adj) Thankful

GRIEVE [GRI-EVE]

(v) To feel sorrow

GRIEVOUS [One I] GRI-EV-OUS]

(adj) Severe

GUANO [GU-AN-O]

> *(n)* Bat or seabird faeces used for fertiliser

GUAVA [GU-AVA]

> *(n)* A tropical fruit

GUIDE [GU-I-DE]

> *(n)* A person, mark or writing that provides information

or

GUILD [GU-ILD]

> *(n)* An association of members

~~guild~~ (gold) → GILD

GUILLOTINE [Hidden U] [GU-ILL-O-TINE]

> Def 1: *(n)* A method of execution; A machine for cutting
>
> Def 2: *(v)* To execute by using a guillotine machine

Gu

GUILT [GU-ILT]

> *(n)* The feeling of having wronged;
>   Having committed or been found to
>   have committed an offence

or

GILT [GIL-T]

> Def 1: *(n)* A thin layer of gold

> Def 2: *(adj)* Covered with a thin layer of
>   gold

Gw

~~gwahno~~ (bat faeces) → GUANO

~~gwahva~~ (fruit) → GUAVA

Gy

GYM [G-Y-M]

> *(n)* A gymnasium;
>   A place for physical activity

H

Ha

HABEAS CORPUS [Latin]

[HA-BEA-S COR-PUS]

(n) A right that protects against unlawful and indefinite imprisonment

HABIT [HAB-IT]

(n) A regular tendency or practice;
An addiction
Religious clothing
or

HABITAT [HAB-IT-AT]

(n) The natural environment of an animal or plant

HABITUÉ [HAB-IT-UÉ]

(n) A resident of or frequent visitor to a particular place

HAEMOGLOBIN [HAE-MO-GLO-BIN]

(n) A protein found in the red blood cells that carries oxygen

Heamoglobin is US English only

Ha

HAEMOPHILIA [One L] [HAE-MO-PHI-LIA]

(n) A condition in which blood does not clot

Hemophillia is US English only

HAEMORRHOID [HAE-MORR-HOID]

(n) A swollen vein near the anus

Heamorrhoid is US English only

HAIKU [Japanese] [Pronounced *hai-cu*] [HAI-KU]

(n) A Japanese poem consisting of:

A first line with 5 syllables

A second line with 7 syllables

A third line with 5 syllables

~~halarious~~ (funny) → HILARIOUS

HALLELUJAH [Hebrew] [HALL-E-LU-JAH]

(n) An expression meaning 'praise the Lord'

Also acceptable is ALLELUJAH

~~halopeno~~ (chili pepper) → JALOPEÑO

HANDKERCHIEF [Hidden D]
[HAND-KER-CHIEF]

(n) A square of material

HANDSOME [Hidden D] [SILENT E]
[HAND-SOM-E]

(adj) Good looking;
Impressive

HANGAR [HANG-AR]

(n) A building used to store aircraft

or

HANGER [HANG-ER]

(n) A hooked device used to hang clothes

HARASS [One R] [HAR-ASS]

(v) To subject to constant pressure or
intimidation

HANUKKAH [Double K] [HAN-U-KK-AH]

(n) A Jewish festival

Ha

HARBOUR [HAR-BOUR]

>   Def 1: *(n)* A place for ships to moor
>
>   Def 2: *(v)* To secretly keep
>
> *or*
>
> ARBOUR [AR-BOUR]
>
>   *(n)* A seat surround by trees

HASTEN [Hidden T] [HASTE-N]

   (v) To hurry

~~haybeas corpus~~ (law) → HABEAS CORPUS

~~haynuss~~ (appalling) → HEINOUS

HAZZARD [No S's] [HAZZ-ARD]

   Def 1: *(n)* A danger

   Def 2: *(v)* To put at risk ;
               To dare to say something

HAZE [No S]

   (n) A thin mist

heamoglobin (blood) → HAEMOGLOBIN
(US English)

heamophillia (blood condition) → HAEMOPHILIA
(US English)

heamorrhoid (swollen vein) → HAEMORRHOID
(US English)

~~heabeas corpus~~ (law) → HABEAS CORPUS

HEAVE [No F] [HE-AVE]

(v) To lift or push with difficulty;
To almost vomit

HEDGEHOG [HEDGE + HOG]

(n) A spikey mammal

HEINOUS [HEIN-OUS]

(adj) Appalling

~~helarious~~ (funny) → HILARIOUS

HERBIVORE [No U] [HEIN-OUS]

(n) An animal that only eats plants

~~heynuss~~ (appalling) → HEINOUS

Hi

Be aware of HY- words as they may incorrectly sound like HI-:

~~hibrid~~ (mixed) → HYBRID

~~hidrate~~ (water) → HYDRATE

~~hidraulic~~ (water) → HYDRAULIC

~~hidrogen~~ (element) → HYDROGEN

~~hiena~~ (animal) → HYENA (or HYAENA)

~~higene~~ (cleanliness) → HYGIENE

~~himn~~ (song) → HYMN

~~hipe~~ (excitement) → HYPE

~~hipnosis~~ (trance) → HYPNOSIS

~~hipocrite~~ (character trait) → HYPOCRITE

~~hipotenuse~~ (triangle) → HYPOTENUSE

~~hipothermia~~ (cold) → HYPOTHERMIA

~~hipothesis~~ (theory) → HYPOTHESIS

~~histerecomy~~ (womb removal) → HYSTERECTOMY

HICCUP [No K] [Double C] [HIC-CUP]

> Def 1: *(n)* An involuntary noise from the diaphragm

> Def 2: *(v)* To make the 'hiccup' sound

~~hiku~~ (Japanese poem) → HAIKU

HILARIOUS [No E] [HIL-AR-IOUS]

(adj) Funny

HIPPOPOTAMUS [Three P's] [HIPPO-POT-TA-MUS]

(adj) A very large mammal

Ho

HOARD [HO-ARD]

Def 1: *(n)* A hidden store

Def 2: *(v)* To collect;
To store

or

HORDE [HOR-DE]

(n) A large group

HOLE [HO-LE]

(n) A hollow in a solid body or surface

or

WHOLE [W-HOLE]

Def 1: *(adj)* Complete

Def 2: *(n)* A thing that is complete

HORIZON [No S] [No E] [HO-RI-ZON]

(n) The line which the earth and the sky
appear to meet

HORRIBLE [Double R] [HOR-RI-BLE]

(adj) Nasty;
Causing horror;
Shocking

Hu

HUNGRY [HUN-GRY]

    (adj) To need food

  vs

HUNGARY [HUNG-ARY]

    (proper noun) A country in Europe

Hy

~~hyatus~~ (break) → HIATUS

HYBRID [HY-BRID]

    (n) Something new created by mixing two or more different things

HYDRATE [HY-DRATE]

    (v) To give water

HYDRAULIC [HY-DRA-U-LIC]

    (adj) Tools and machinery worked by water pressure

Hy

HYDROGEN [HY-DRO-GEN]

(n) An elemental gas

| Chemical Element Symbol = **H** |
| Atomic Number = **1** |

HYENA [HY-ENA]

(n) An African canine, stereotypically known for laughing

Also acceptable is HYAENA

HYGIENE [Hidden I] [HY-GI-ENE]

(n) Keeping clean to prevent illness or smells

HYMN [HY-MN]

(n) A religious song

HYPE [HY-PE]

(v) To draw attention and excitement to

HYPNOSIS [HYP-NO-SIS]

(n) A practice in which a person is placed in a trance where they become susceptible to instructions

HYPOCRITE [HYPO-CRIT-E]

(n) A person who does the opposite of what they say

HYPODERMIC [HYPO-DER-MIC]

Def 1: *(n)* A syringe

Def 2: *(adj)* To inject underneath the skin

HYPOTENUSE [HYPO-TEN-USE]

(n) The longest side of a triangle

HYPOTHERMIA [HYPO-THER-MIA]

(n) Dangerously low body temperature

HYPOTHESIS [HYPO-THE-SIS]

(n) A theory that has not been proven

HYPOTHESIZE [HYPO-THE-SIZE]

(v) To create a theory

Also acceptable is HYPOTHESISE

HYPOTHETICAL [HYPO-THE-TICAL]

(adj) Based on possible situations

Hy

HYSTERECTOMY [HYS-TER-REC-TO-MY]

(n) To remove the womb

HYSTERIA [HYS-TER-IA]

(n) Uncontrolled emotion

I

Ic

ICICLE [Not ICE-] [I-CI-CLE]
> *(n)* A hanging piece of ice

Id

~~idillic~~ (perfect) → IDYLLIC

IDIOCY [No T] [IDI-O-CY]
> *(n)* Stupid

IDIOT [ID-I-OT]
> *(n)* A stupid person

IDYLLIC [Pronounced *i-dill-ic*] [I-DYL-LIC]
> *(adj)* Ideal;
>> A perfect situation

IL

iland (surrounded by sea) → ISLAND

ile (island) → ISLE

ILLEGITIMATE [IL-LEGIT- I-MATE]

(adj) Not allowed (e.g: by law);
A child born out of marriage

ILLICIT [Double L] [ILL-I-CIT]

(adj) Unlawful;
Rude

vs

ELICIT [EL-LI-CIT]

(v) To draw a reaction

irrelevant (not connected) → IRRELEVANT

ilterate (repeat) → ITERATE

IMAGINE [IM-AG-INE]

> *(v)* To form a mental image;
> To assume

imbarrass (shame) → EMBARRASS

IMMACULATE [Double M] [IM-MAC-U-LATE]

> *(adj)* Free from flaws or sins;
> Perfect

IMMENSE [Double M] [IM-MEN-SE]

> *(adj)* Extremely large

IMPLAUSIBLE [IM-PLAUS-I-BLE]

> *(n)* Unlikely;
> Not convincing

IMPLICATE [No E] [IM-PLI-CATE]

> *(v)* To attach to a crime

IMPLICATION [IM-PLAUS-I-BLE]

> *(n)* The conclusion that can be drawn from,
> without explicitly stating

Im

IMPLY [IMPLY]

> *(v)* To suggest something without directly
> stating it

vs

INFER [IN-FER]

> *(v)* To work out using evidence

IMPORTANTLY [Middle -ANT-] [IM-PORT-ANT-LY]

(adv) Used to emphasize a point

IMPOSSIBLE [No N] [IM-POSS-I-BLE]

(adj) Not being able to exist to achieve

IMPRESS [MP-RESS]

> *(v)* To make someone feel admiration;
> To push a design or mark in

vs

EMPRESS [EMP-RESS]

> *(n)* A female ruler

IMPUGN [Pronounced *in-puw-ne*] [IM-PU-GN]

(v) To express doubts about honesty

~~inbryo~~ (undeveloped) → EMBRYO

INCIDENT [IN-CI-DENT]

>*(n)* An event

INCISOR [IN-CIS-OR]

>*(n)* A type of tooth

INCLINATION [No E] [IN-CLI-NATION]

>*(n)* A person's natural tendency to do something

INCOGNITO [Pronounced *in-kog-nito*] [IN-COG-NI-TO]

>*(adj) (adv)* Disguised in order to avoid being recognised

INDEPENDENT [IN-DE-PEND-ENT]

>*(adj)* Free from outside influence

INDICT [Pronounced *in-dyte*] [IN-DI-CT]

>*(v)* To formally charge (to accuse of a crime)

INDIGO [No E] [IN-DI-GO]

>*(n)* A bark blue, purplish colour

In

INDISTINCT [IN-DIS-TIN-CT]

(adj) Not clear

INDIVIDUAL [No E] [IN-DI-VID-U-AL]

(adj) Single;
Unique

INDUSTRY [IN-DUST-RY]

(n) The manufacture of goods;
Areas providing services

INEFFABLE [IN-EFF-ABLE]

(adj) Cannot be described

INEQUITABLE [IN-E-QUIT-ABLE]

(adj) Unfair

INERTIA [Pronounced *in-er-sha*] [IN-ERT-IA]

(n) The characteristic not to move unless
external forces are applied

INEVITABLE [IN-EVIT-ABLE]

(adj) Certain to happen;
Cannot be stopped

INEXHAUSTIBLE [IN-EX-HAUST-I-BLE]

(adj) Unlimited quantities

INFER [IN-FER]

(v) To work out using evidence

vs

IMPLY [IMPLY]

(v) To suggest something without directly stating it

INFINITE [IN-FIN-ITE]

(adj) Limitless

INFINITY [IN-FIN-ITY]

(n) Unlimited and never ending

INFRARED [Not *infer*- [IN-FRA-RED]

(adj) (n) A wavelength of electromagnetic radiation

INFRASTRUCTURE [IN-FRA-STRUCT-URE]

(n) The structures and facilities required by a society

INFURIATE [IN-FUR-I-ATE]

(v) To cause anger

In

INGEST [No J] [IN-GEST]

(v) To eat or drink something

INNOCENT [Double N] [IN-NO-CENT]

Def 1: *(adj)* Not guilty;
Having little experience;
Naïve

Def 2: *(n)* A person who has done no wrong

INTEGRATE [Not *inter-*] [IN-TE-GRATE]

(v) To combine;
To accept into a group

INTEREST [IN-TER-EST]

Def 1: *(n)* Eagerness;
Money paid on top of a loan

Def 2: *(v)* To be curious

INUIT [IN-U-IT]

(n) The native people of the Arctic regions

INVERTEBRATE [IN-VER-E-BRATE]

(n) An animal without a backbone

IRRELEVANT [Double R] [Ending -ANT]
[IR-RELE-VANT]

(adj) Not connected

ISLAND [Pronounced *i-land*] [IS-LAND]

(n) Land surrounded by water

vs

IRELAND [IRE-LAND]

(proper noun) A country in Europe

ISLE [IS-LE]

(n) An Island

ISOSCELES [Pronounced *i-soss-i-leeze*]
[I-SOS-CE-LES]

(adj) A triangle with 2 equal sides

It

ITERATE [IT-ER-ATE]

(v) To perform or utter repeatedly

J

Ja

JACKBOOT [JACK+BOOT]

(n) A protective military boot reaching the knee

JACOBITE [JAC-O-BITE]

(cap) (n) A supporter of King James II after his deposition

JALAPEÑO [JAL-A-PEÑ-O]

(n) A type of chilli Pepper

JAMBOREE [JAM-BO-REE]

(n) A party or large gathering

JANITOR [No E] [JAN-I-TOR]

(n) A caretaker

JAUNDICE [Not *jawn-*] [JA-UN-DI-CE]

(n) Yellowing of the skin

Je

JEHOVAH [JE-HOV-AH]

(cap) (n) Another name for God in the bible

JEOPARDY [Not *jepo-*] [JEO-PARD-Y]

(n) Danger

JETTISON [No ER] [JETT-I-SON]

(v) To throw from a vehicle

JEWELLERY [JEWELL-ER-Y]

(n) Personal ornaments worn on the body

Jewelery is US English only

~~jigalo~~ (escort) → GIGOLO

JIHAD [Arabic] [JI-HAD]

(n) A Muslim war against non-believers

JILT [JI-LT]

(v) To unexpectedly abandon

JINX [JIN-X]

Def 1: *(n)* Something that brings bad luck

Def 2: *(v)* To curse;
To bring bad luck to

~~jist~~ (sense) → GIST

Jo

JODHPURS [Not jop-] [JOD-H-PURS]

(pl) (n) Trousers worn for horse riding

JOIST [JO-I-ST]

(n) A supporting beam

JOULE [JO-U-LE]

(n) A unit of energy

> *The shortened form is **J***

JOWL [No E] [JO-WL]

(n) The lower section of the cheek

JUBILEE [JU-BI-LEE]

(n) A special anniversary

JUGGERNAUT [JUGGER-NA-UT]

Def 1: *(adj)* Large; Powerful;
Difficult to beat

Def 2: *(n)* A vehicle

JUGULAR [JUG-U-LAR]

(n) Veins in the neck

JU-JITSU [Japanese] [JU - JIT-SU]

(n) Unarmed combat

JUNCTURE [JUN-CT-URE]

(n) A point in time;
Where things meet

JUNIOR [Ending -IOR] [JUN-I-OR]

Def 1: *(adj)* Younger;
Schoolchildren;
Son;
Lower ranked

Def 2: *(n)* A younger person;
A schoolchild

Ju

JUXTAPOSE [JUX-TA-POSE]

(v) To place close together

K

Be aware of C words as they may sound like they start with K.

Here are some examples:

~~karisma~~ (charm) → CHARISMA

~~kaveat~~ (warning) → CAVEAT

~~kernal~~ (rank) → COLONEL

~~kokicx~~ (bone) → COCCYX

~~konstonant~~ (word) → CONSONANT

~~konsumate~~ (marriage) → CONSUMMATE

~~koo~~ (take power) → COUP

~~koopay~~ (car) → COUPE

~~kornal~~ (officer rank) → COLONEL

~~korpreal~~ (rank) → CORPORAL

Ka

kabab (food) → KEBAB

kaki (colour) → KHAKI

KALEIDOSCOPE [KA-LIE-DO-SCOPE]

(n) Brightly coloured changing patterns

KAMIKAZE [Japanese] [KAM-I-KAZE]

(adj) To destroy others along with yourself;
Reckless

KANGAROO [KANG-A-ROO]

(n) A large marsupial from Australia

KARAOKE [Japanese] [KAR-A-O-KE]

(n) Entertainment where people sing songs

KARATE [Japanese] [KAR-ATE]

(n) Unarmed combat

karnavor (meat eater) → CARNIVORE

KARMA [KAR-MA]

(n) (In Buddhism and Hinduism) The belief
persons actions affects their fate;
Consequences

KEBAB [KE-BAB]

(n) Meat on skewers

~~kee~~ (shipping) → QUAY

~~keesh~~ (food) → QUICHE

KERB [K-ERB]

(n) The edge of a pavement

Curb is US English only

KERFUFFLE [KER-FUFFLE]

(n) Commotion;
A fuss

KERNEL [KER-NEL]

(n) The softer part of a seed or nut;
Essential

or

COLONEL [COL-O-NEL]

(n) An Army rank

Ke

~~kerput~~ (broken) → KAPUT

KETCHUP [KET-CH-UP]
> *(n)* Tomato sauce

~~keyosk~~ (booth) → KIOSK

~~keywe~~ (fruit) → KIWI

~~keworum~~ (minimum number) → QUORUM

Kh

KHAKI [KH-A-KI]
> *(n)* A dull green-yellow colour

KILOMETRE [KILO+ METRE]

(n) A unit of measurement equal to 1000 metres

> *The shortened form is* ***km***

Kilometer is US English only

> 1.6 km (or 1600 metres) is equivalent to a mile

KIOSK [KI-O-SK]

(n) A booth from which things are sold or given

KITCHEN [KIT-CHEN]

(n) A room in which people primarily cook

KITTEN [Double T] [KIT-TEN]

(n) A young cat or feline

KIWI [KI-WI]

(n) A type of fruit;
A bird from New Zealand;
(informal) A person from New Zealand

Kn

KNAPSACK [Silent K] [K-NAP-SACK]

(n) A small bag

KNEAD [Silent K] [K-NEAD]

(v) To work dough or clay;
To massage

or

NEED [N-EED]

Def 1: *(v)* To want something as it is essential

Def 2: *(n)* Something that is needed;
Being required to do something

KNEE [Silent K] [K-NEE]

(n) The largest joint in the leg

KNEEL [Silent K] [K-NEE-L]

(v) To get on your knee(s)

KNEW [K-NEW]

> *(v)* The past tense of to KNOW

or

NEW [N-EW]

> *(n)* Recently created, birthed or made;
> Not previously used or owned

KNICKERS [Silent K] [K-NICK-ERS]

> *(n)* Girls underwear

KNIFE [Silent K] [K-NIFE]

> Def 1: *(n)* A bladed cutting tool with a handle
>
> Def 2: *(v)* To stab with a knife

KNIGHT [Silent K] [K-NIGHT]

> Def 1: *(n)* A high ranking medieval fighter;
> A sir;
> A chess piece that moves in a 'L' shape
>
> *or*

NIGHT [N-IGHT]

> *(n)* The period of time from sunset to sunrise

Kn

KNIT [Silent K] [K-NIT]

    (v) To make by connecting yarn

vs

NIT [N-IT]

    (n) The egg of a louse

KNOB [Silent K] [K-NOB]

    (n) A handle;
        A round lump

KNOCK [Silent K] [K-NOCK]

    Def 1: *(v)* To tap to get attention;
        To hit or destroy

    Def 2: *(n)* A setback;
        A tapping noise

KNOLL [Silent K] [K-NOLL]

    (n) A small hill

KNOT [K-NOT]

(n) A fastening;
A tightening;
A tangled mass;
A hard mass within a tree;
A maritime unit of speed

or

NOT [N-OT]

(n) Forbid;
Negative

KNOW [Silent K] [Silent W] [K-NOW]

(v) To be aware of;
To be certain

KNOWLEDGE [No A] [Silent K] [K-NOW-LEDGE]

(n) Information;
Experience

KNOWN [Silent K] [K-NOWN]

Def 1: *(v)* The past tense of KNOW

Def 2: *(adj)* Recognised

KNUCKLE [Silent K] [K-NUCK-LE]

(n) A joint on a finger or toe

Ko

KOALA [KO-A-LA]

(n) A bear like marsupial native to Australia

KOI [Pronounced *koy*] [No Y] [K-OI]

(n) A large Japanese fish

KOSHER [Hebrew] [No H] [KO-SHER]

(adj) Created in accordance with Jewish customs;
(informal) Legitimate

Ku

kuhrisma (charm) → CHARISMA

kuhtastrophe (disaster) → CATASTROPHE

Kw

kwasar (galaxy) → QUASAR

kwell (suppress) → QUELL

kwiry (question) → QUERY

kwis (test) → QUIZ

L

La

LABEL [Ending -EL] [LAB-EL]

    Def 1: *(v)* To attach information

    Def 2: *(n)* Attached information;
             Stereotype

vs

LAPEL [Ending -EL] [LAP-EL]

    (n) A label on clothing

LABIA [No Y] [LA-B-IA]

    (pl) (n) Folds of skin around the vaginal
        opening

LABOUR [Hidden U] [LA-B-OUR]

    Def 1: *(n)* Work;
            Childbirth

    Def 2: *(v)* To do work;
            To move with difficulty

   Labor is US English only

La

LABRADOR [One O] [LAB-RA-DOR]

(cap) (n) A breed of dog

LABYRINTH [Hidden Y] [LAB-Y-RIN-TH]

(n) A complicated maze

LACKADAISICAL [LACK-A-DAIS-I-CAL]

(adj) Careless;
Uninspired

LACKLUSTRE [Ending in -RE]
[LACK-LUST-RE]

(adj) Lacking in energy or enthusiasm;
Dull

LACONIC [LA-CON-IC]

(adj) Using few words

LACQUER [Hidden -QU-] [No K] [LAC-QU-ER]

Def 1: *(n)* Varnish

Def 2: *(n)* To coat with varnish

LACTATE [No K] [LAC-TATE]

(v) To produce milk naturally

LAGER [One R] [LAG-ER]

(n) A type of beer

~~lama~~ (animal) → LLAMA

LAMB [Ending with a silent B] [LAM-B]

Def 1: *(n)* A young sheep

Def 2: *(v)* To give birth or to help a sheep give birth to a lamb

LANGUAGE [Hidden U] [LAN-GU-AGE]

(n) Communication;
Rules written for a computer

LANGUISH [Hidden U] [LAN-GU-ISH]

(v) To leave waiting;
To become weak

La

LAPEL [Ending -EL] [LAP-EL]

    (n) A label on clothing

vs

LABEL [Ending -EL] [LAB-EL]

    Def 1: *(v)* To attach information

    Def 2: *(n)* Attached information;
                Stereotype

LAPSE [No C] [LAP-SE]

    Def 1: *(v)* Failure to do something due to a lack
            of concentration;
            Decline in standards;
            Time difference

    Def 2: *(n)* Attached information;
                Stereotype

~~larger~~ (beer) → LAGER

LARYNGITIS [No E] [Hidden Y]
             [LAR-YN-GITIS]

    (n) When the vocal cords in the throat become
    swollen

LASAGNA [Italian] [LAS-A-GNA]

(n) Pasta sheets layered with meat and sauce

Also acceptable is LASAGNE

LASSO [No Z's] [LA-SS-O]

Def 1: *(n)* A rope for catching cattle

Def 2: *(v)* To catch with a lasso

LATTE [Pronounced *lat-tay*] [LAT-TE]

(n) A type of milky coffee

LAUD [No W] [L-AUD]

(v) To praise

LAUNDERETTE [LAUNDER-ETTE]

(n) A public place to wash clothes

LAWYER [LAW-YER]

(n) A person who practises law

Le

LEACH [LEA-CH]

(v) To empty, drain or remove.

vs

LEECH [LEE-CH]

Def 1: *(n)* A bloodsucking worm

Def 2: *(v)* To take resources from without equity

LEAF [LEA-F]

Def 1: *(n)* A flat part of a plant growing from
the stem;
A single page;
A thin sheet of metal

Def 2: *(v)* To flick through

The plural is LEAVES

~~leater~~ (liquid weight) → LITRE

LEAVE [LE-A-VE]

(v) To go away from;
To quit

The plural is LEAVES

~~lefel~~ (position) → LEVEL

LEGEND [LEG + END]

(n) A traditional story intended to be regarded as historical but is not authenticated; A famous person

LEISURE [LEI-SURE]

(n) Time for relaxing

LEITMOTIF [Starting LEI-] [LE-I-T-MO-TIF]

(n) Frequently repeated themes within music

LEMUR [LE-MUR]

(n) A primate found in Madagascar

LENGTH [LEN-GTH]

(n) Measurements

LEPRECHAUN [LEP-RE-CH-AUN]

(n) (fantasy) An Irish elf-like being

LESBIAN [LES-B-IAN]

(n) Women who are attracted exclusively to other women

Le

LETHAL [No F] [LE-THAL]

(adj) Deadly

LETTUCE [Double T] [LET-TUCE]

(n) A vegetable

LEUKAEMIA [LE-UK-AE-MIA]

(n) A type of blood cancer that affects blood cells in the bone marrow

Leukemia is US English only

LEVEE [No I] [LE-VEE]

(n) An embankment built to defend against flooding

LEVITATE [LEV-I-TATE]

(v) To hover

~~lezanya~~ (food) → LASAGNA / LASAGNE

LIBRARY [Hidden R] [LIB-R-ARY]

(n) A building or room used to house books

LICENCE [No S] [LI-CEN-CE]

(n) Permission to own or do something

License is US English only

LICENSE [With a S] [LI-CEN-SE]

(v) To give a licence

Also acceptable is LICENCE

LICHEN [Pronounced *ly-ken*] [LI-CHEN]

(n) A fungus plant that resembles moss

~~licee~~ (spikey fruit) → LYCHEE

~~lickwid~~ (fluid) → LIQUID

LIECHTENSTEIN [LIE-CH-TEN-STEIN]

(proper noun) A country in Europe

~~liesure~~ (relax) → LEISURE

LIEU [Pronounced *loo*] [L-I-UE]

(n) Instead

Li

LIEUTENANT [Pronounced *left-ten-ant*]
[LIEU + TENANT]

(n) A rank in the Army and Navy

Note: In US English it is pronounced 'loo-ten-ant'

LIGHTNING [No E] [Middle N] [LIGHT-N-ING]

(n) A natural discharge of electricity in the atmosphere

LIKELIHOOD [LIKE-LI-HOOD]

(n) The probability of something happening

LIMB [Ending in a silent B] [LIM-B]

(n) Growing from but still connected to something;
An arm, leg, wing or branch

Be careful of LY and LI confusion.
The main examples of this are:

~~lieing~~ (to lie) → LYING

~~linch~~ (to kill) → LYNCH

~~linx~~ (animal) → LYNX

~~liric~~ (music) → LYRIC

LIQUEFY [LI-QU-E-FY]

(v) To turn to liquid

LIQUEUR [Hidden U] [LIQU-E-UR]

(n) A type of alcohol

LIQUID [No C] [LI-QU-ID]

(n) A state of mass in which something flows

LIQUORICE [LI-QUOR-ICE]

(n) A black sweet;
A plant

Licorice is US English only

LITRE [LI-T-RE]

(n) One thousand millilitres

Liter is US English only

LITERALLY [One T] [LIT-ER-ALLY]

(n) The original meaning of a word or phrase
with no exaggeration;
Used to emphasize without being intended
to be seen as truthful

LI

LLAMA [Double L] [LL-AMA]

(n) A South American woolly animal

Lo

LOGIC [No D] [LO-G-IC]

(n) Reasoning based on evidence

LONELY [LONE-LY]

(n) Sadness due to being alone; Remote

~~loo~~ (instead (e.g.: in loo off)) → LIEU

LOOFA [LOO-FA]

(n) Part of a dried tropical fruit used as a bathroom sponge

~~lookemia~~ (blood cancer) → LEUKAEMIA

~~loyer~~ (law) → LAWYER

~~luhsanya~~ (food) → LASAGNA / LASAGNE

LUMINESCENCE [LUM-IN-ES-CENCE]

> *(n)* Light given from substances in ways other than heat

LUSTRE [Ending in -RE] [LUST-RE]

> *(n)* The brightness that a shiny surface has; Prestige

> *Luster* is US English only

LUXURY [Double U] [No E] [LY-NX]

> *(n)* Comfortable;
> Expensive;
> Not needed for survival

Ly

LYCHEE [No I] [LY-CHEE]

(n) A spikey skinned fruit

LYING [No I] [LY-ING]

(v) To not tell the truth

~~lyken~~ (fungi plant) → LICHEN

~~lymotif~~ (music) → LEITMOTIF

LYNCH [No I] [LY-N-CH]

(v) To kill without a legal trial, usually by a mob

LYNX [No I] [LY-NX]

(n) A wild cat

LYRIC [No I] [LY-RIC]

(n) Words of a song

M

Ma

MA'AM [Separated by an apostrophe] [ma- '- am]

(n) A respectful form of address to a woman

MACABRE [Ending -RE] [MAC-AB-RE]

(n) Overly interested in death or injury

MACHETE [MA-CH-ETE]

(n) A large knife

MACHIAVELLIAN [MACH-IA-VELL-IAN]

(adj) Cunning;
Playing both sides to gain an advantage

MACKEREL [Ending -EL] [MACK-ER-EL]

(n) A sea fish

MAELSTROM [MA-EL-STROM]

(n) A whirlpool;
A confusing situation

MAESTRO [MAE-STRO]

(n) Exceptionally talented, particularly in classical music

Ma

MAGAZINE [Middle A] [MAG-A-ZINE]

(n) A print published at regular intervals;
An object used to hold ammunition rounds
before firing

MADAM [No E] [MAD-AM]

(n) A respectful and polite address about
or for a woman

or

MADAME [Pronounced *muh-dam*] [MAD-AME]

(n) (cap) A title for a French woman

MAGGOT [Double G] [MAG-GOT]

(n) The larva of an insect

MAIDEN [MA-CH-ETE]

Def 1: *(n)* A innocent woman

Def 2: *(adj)* The first of its kind;
An unmarried woman

MAIM [MA-IM]

(v) To permanently injury

MAINTAIN [NO E] [MAIN-TAIN]

(n) To continue;
    To check and repair regularly;
    To support

MAINTENANCE [With two E's]
[MAIN-TEN-ANCE]

(n) To continue;
    To check and repair regularly;
    To support

MAISONETTE [MAI-SON-ETTE]

(n) A flat spread over two levels

MAÎTRE D'HÔTEL [French]
[MAÎ-TRE D'HÔTEL]

(n) A head waiter

Translates to 'Master of the House'

Normally shortened to MAÎTRE D

~~maitron~~ (woman supervisor) → MATRON

Ma

MAIZE [Middle I] [MA-I-ZE]

> *(n)* A plant whose grains are used in cereals

> *vs*

MAZE [MA-ZE]

> *(n)* A network of paths and hedges with one exit designed as a puzzle

MAJOR [MAJ-OR]

> Def 1: *(adj)* Important ;
>   Main;
>   Relating to musical scales

> Def 2: *(n)* A rank in the army

> Def 3: *(v)* To specialise in (US collages)

MALEVOLENT [Pronounced *muh-lev-o-lent*]
         [MAL-E-VO-LENT]

> *(adj)* Wishing harm on others

MALICIOUS [MAL-I-COUS]

> *(adj)* Wishing to harm others

MALIGN [Pronounced *muh-lyn*] [MAL-IGN]

Def 1: *(adj)* Evil

Def 2: *(n)* Speak about in a spiteful manner

MAMMAL [MAM-MAL]

(n) An animal that is warm blooded, produced milk and births live young

MANOEUVRE [MAN-OEU-VRE]

Def 1: *(n)* A skilled movement;
A well-planned action

Def 2: *(v)* To move with skill or care;
To manipulate

MANOR [MAN-OR]

(n) A large house in the countryside with lands

MANUAL [Middle U] [MAN-U-AL]

Def 1: *(adj)* Needed to be operated in person;
Working with hands

Def 2: *(n)* A guide or instruction book

Ma

MANUFACTURE [MAN-U-FACTURE]

Def 1: *(adj)* Make on a large scale;
Invent a story

Def 2: *(v)* To manufacture

MARATHON [Not -*ph*-] [MAR-A-THON]

(n) A long-distance foot race

MARIJUANA [MAR-I-JU-ANA]

(n) Cannabis

MARQUESS [MAR-QUESS]

(n) A rank in an aristocracy system

MARSUPIAL [MAR-SUP-IAL]

(n) A mammal who's young are carried and
suckled in a pouch

MARTYR [No E] [MAR-TYR]

Def 1: *(n)* A person killed for their beliefs

Def 2: *(v)* To posthumously enhance
someone's by killing them for their
beliefs

MASOCHISM [MA-SCO-CH-ISM]

(n) Enjoyment of your own pain or humiliation

MASTERPIECE [MASTER+ PIECE]

(n) Outstanding

MASTURBATE [No ER] [Middle U]
[MAST-UR-BATE]

(v) To self-simulate genitals

MATERIAL [MATER-IAL]

Def 1: *(n)* What something is made from;
Cloth

Def 2: *(adj)* Relevant;
Relating to physical matter

MATHEMATICS [Middle E] [MATH-E-MATICS]

(n) Relating to the study of numbers;
Equations

MATRIARCH [MA-TRI-ARCH]

(n) The female ruler of a family or group

~~matra d~~' (waiter) → MAÎTRE D ('HÔTEL)

Ma

MATRON [MA-TRON]

(n) An older married woman;
A woman in charge of medical and living
arrangements at a school or hospital;
(British English) A woman in charge of
nursing in a hospital ward

MATTRESS [Double T] [MATT-RESS]

(n) A comfy object for sleeping on

MAUL [MA-UL]

(v) To wound;
To treat roughly

MAUSOLEUM [Not *maw*-] [MAU-SOL-EUM]

(n) A building containing tombs

Ma

Be careful of confusing MAY with other MA- words.

The main examples of this are:

~~mayden~~ (innocent) → MAIDEN

~~maylstrom~~ (whirlpool) → MAELSTROM

~~maytain~~ (continue) → MAINTAIN

~~maytra d~~ (head waiter) → MAÎTRE (D'HÔTEL)

~~mayjestic~~ (beautiful) → MAJESTIC

~~mayjor~~ (important) → MAJESTIC

~~maytriarche~~ (head woman) → MATRIARCH

~~maytron~~ (woman supervisor) → MATRON

Me

MEAGRE [Ending -RE] [MEA-GRE]

(n) A small amount

Meager is US English only

MEASURE [MEA-SUR-E]

Def 1: *(v)* To find the size or amount of
something;
To reach a certain standard

Def 2: *(n)* A proposed law;
An action in response to something

MECHANIC [Hidden H] [ME-CHAN-IC]

(n) A person who fixes machines, including
vehicles

~~mechete~~ (knife) → MACHETE

MEDICINE [Middle I] [MED-I-CINE]

(n) The science and practice of human
healthcare;
A substance taken to help with ailments

MEDICINAL [MEDIC-IN-AL]

Def 1: *(adj)* Having healing properties

Def 2: *(n)* Medicine

MEDIA [One A at the end] [ME-D-IA]

>   *(n)* The means of mass communication
>   (e.g.: broadcasting)

>   Note: Media is also the plural of MEDIUM

MEDIOCRE [Middle I] [Not -*core*]
[MED-IO-CRE]

>   *(adj)* Slightly boring due to being average

MEDIUM [Middle I] [MED-I-UM]

>   Def 1: *(n)* The middle between two points;
>   A psychic;
>   A substance in which something is
>   conveyed

>   Def 2: *(adj)* Between two extremes

MELEE [Pronounced *mel-ay*] [ME-LEE]

>   *(n)* An unorganised fight;
>   A confused group

MEMOIR [Pronounced *mem-war*] [MEM-OIR]

>   *(n)* A written account about personal
>   knowledge of events

~~merr~~ (incense) → MYRRH

Me

METAPHOR [No -ER] [META-PH-OR]

(n) A word or phrase not intended to be taken literally

METRE [Ending -RE] [MET-RE]

(n) A metric distance equivalent to 100 cm;
The basic rhythmic structure of a poem

> *The shortened form is* **m**

Meter is US English only

MEZZANINE [MEZZ-AN-INE]

(n) A floor in a building that is open to the floor below

Mi

MIDDLE [Double D] [Ending in -LE] [MI-DD-LE]

Def 1: *(adj)* An equal distance between two points

Def 2: *(n)* The centre

MIDGE [MID-GE]

(n) A small biting flying insect

MILLENNIUM [Double L] Double N] [MILL-ENN-IUM]

(n) One thousand years

MILLI- [MILL-I] Relates to a Thousand

MILLIGRAM [MILL-I-GRAM]

(n) One thousandth of a grams

> *The shortened form is **mg***

MILLILITRE [MILL-I-LITRE]

(n) One thousandth of a litre

> *The shortened form is **ml***

US English only is MILLILITER

MILLIMETRE [MILL-I-MET-RE]

(n) One thousandth of a metre

> *The shortened form is **mm***

US English only is MILLIMETER

MILLION [MILL-ION]

(n) One thousand thousand (1 000 000)

MILLISECOND [MILL-I-SECOND]

> *The shortened form is **ms***

(n) One thousandth of a second

Mi

MILLIPEDE [MILL-I-PEDE]

(n) A small animal with many legs

MINUSCULE [Hidden U] [MIN-U-SC-ULE]

(n) Tiny

MINUTE [Pronounced *min-it*] [MIN-U-TE]

Def 1: *(n)* A unit of time equal to sixty seconds;
Formal summary notes taken about
a meeting

Def 2: *(v)* To take formal summary notes

is spelt the same as

MINUTE [Pronounced *my-noot*] [MIN-U-TE]

(n) Tiny;
Careful and precise

~~miomatosis~~ (rabbit disease) → MYXOMATOSIS

MIRACLE [MIR-A-CLE]

(n) A remarkable yet welcome event, perhaps
attributed to a god, goddess or saint

~~miriad~~ (a great amount) → MYRIAD

MIRE [MI-RE]

(n) A boggy area

Be careful of confusing MIS- with MISS.
The MIS- prefix only has one S

(MIS + the original word)

MISADVENTURE [MIS + ADVENTURE]

MISFIRE [MIS + FIRE]

MISFORTUNE [MIS + FORTUNE]

MISJUDGE [MIS + JUDGE]

MISMATCH [MIS + MATCH]

MISPLACE [MIS + PLACE]

MISQUOTE [MIS + QUOTE]

MISSHAPEN [Double S] [MIS + SHAPEN]

MISSPELL [Double S] [MIS + SPELL]

MISTAKE [MIS + TAKE]

MISUSE [MIS + USE]

Mi

MISCELLANEOUS [No ending E]
[MISC-ELL-AN-EO-US]

(adj) Involving different types

MISCHIEVOUS [Ending in -ous]
[MIS-CHIE-VOUS]
(adj) Naughty;
Intending to cause trouble

MISOGYNIST [MIS-OGY-NIST]

(n) A man who hates women

~~misomatosis~~ (rabbit disease) → MYXOMATOSIS

MISSILE [Hidden I] [MISS-I-LE]

(n) An object thrown or fired at something

MISSION [MISS-ION]

(n) An important aim

MISTLETOE [Starting MIST-] [MIST-LE-TOE]

(n) A white berried plant that people traditionally kiss underneath

~~mistery~~ (unknown) → MYSTERY

~~mistic~~ (magic) → MYSTIC

MITIGATE [No middle E] [MITI-GATE]

(n) Reduce impact and severity

~~mith~~ (unproven) → MYTH

MNEMONIC [Silent M at the start] [M-NEM-ON-IC]

(n) A word or letter patterns to help remember things

Mo

MOIST [No E] [MO-IST]

(adj) Damp

MONARCH [MON-ARCH]

(n) A king or queen

MONGREL [MON-GREL]

(n) A dog of no definable type or breed

MONSIEUR [French] [MON-SIE-UR]

(n) *(cap)* A title for a French man

MONTH [No E] [MON-TH]

(n) One of twelve periods of time that make up a year

MORAL [No E] [MO-RAL]

(n) Relating to if something is ethically right or wrong

or

MORALE [MO-RAL-E]

(n) The confidence, enthusiasm, happiness and discipline levels of a person or group

MORGUE [Hidden U] [MOR-GUE]

> *(n)* A place where recently deceased people are kept before burial

---

MORNING [No U] [MORN-ING]

> *(n)* The period of time between daybreak and noon

or

MOURNING [MOURN-ING]

> *(n)* Sorrow for a death or loss

MORPHINE [No F] [MOR-PH-INE]

> *(adj)* A painkiller

~~morsoleum~~ (tomb) → MAUSOLEUM

MOSQUE [MOS-QUE]

> *(n)* A Muslim place of worship

MOSTLY [No E] [MOST-LY]

> *(adv)* Mainly

Mo

MOTOR [MOT-OR]

Def 1: *(n)* A machine supplying power;
An informal term for a car

Def 2: *(adj)* Giving or production motion

Def 3: *(v)* To travel by car

~~motzarella~~ (cheese) → MOZZARELLA

MOULD [Hidden U] [MO-U-LD]

Def 1: *(n)* Fungi growth;
A container in which certain liquids
are shaped

Def 2: *(n)* To shape;
To influence

Mold is US English only

MOULT [Hidden U] [MO-U-LT]

(n) To shed hairs or feathers

MOURNING [MOURN-ING]

(n) Sorrow for a death or loss

or

MORNING [No U] [MORN-ING]

(n) The period of time between daybreak and noon

MOUSSE [Hidden U] [MO-U-SSE]

(n) A creamy food that incorporates air bubbles to give it light and airy texture; A foam that you put in your hair

MOUSTACHE [Hidden U] [MO-UST-ACH-E]

(n) Hair above the lip

Mustache is US English only

MOZZARELLA [MOZZ-AR-ELLA]

(n) A type of cheese

Mu

~~mual~~ (injure) → MAUL

MUESLI [Hidden E] [MU-E-SLI]

> *(n)* A type of breakfast cereal

~~muhnoeuvre~~ (movement) → MANOEUVRE

~~muhshete~~ (knife) → MACHETE

~~murr~~ (incense) → MYRRH

~~mursoleum~~ (tomb) → MAUSOLEUM

MUSCLE [MUS-CLE]

> Def 1: *(n)* Body tissue consisting of long cells
> that produce motion

> Def 2: *(v)* To move

mustache (lip hair) → MOUSTACHE
(US English)

MUSEUM [MUSE-UM]

> *(n)* A building in which objects of importance
> interest are kept

MUTUAL [MUT-U-AL]

> *(adj)* Shared equally

~~myre~~ (bog) → MIRE

MYRIAD [MY-RI-AD]

(adj) A large number of something

MYRRH [Pronounced *murr*] [MY-RR-H]

(adj) A scented resin, given along with frankincense and gold at the nativity

MYSTERY [MY-STER-Y]

(n) Unexplained

MYSTERIOUS [MY-STER-IOUS]

(n) Something that cannot be explained

MYSTIC [MY-ST-IC]

(n) Someone who attempts to communicate with God through prayer;
Relating to magic or having magic powers

~~mystro~~ (talented) → MAESTRO

My

MYTH [MY-TH]

> *(n) (folklore)* Tradition stories without proof;
> Widley believed but untrue

MYTHOLOGY [MY-TH-OLO-GY]

> *(n)* A collection of myths

MYXOMATOSIS [MY-XO-MATO-SIS]

> *(n)* A disease found in rabbits

N

Na

NAAN [NA-AN]

(n) An Indian flatbread

Also acceptable is NAN

~~nacessiry~~ (needed) → NECESSARY

~~naglect~~ (uncared for) → NEGLECT

NAIVE [NA-I-VE]

(adj) Lacking experience;
Innocence

NAKED [NA-KED]

(adj) Without clothes;
Open and visible

NAN [NA-N]

(n) (informal) A grandmother;
An Indian flatbread (also known as NANN)

NAPALM [NA-PALM]

(adj) An incendiary mixture used in firebombs

Na

NARCISSIUM [NAR-CISS-IUM]

> *(adj)* Where a person has an unreasonably high sense of their own importance

NARRATE [Double R] [NA-RR-ATE]

> *(v)* To provide commentary;
> To tell a story

NATIVITY [NA-TIV-ITY]

> *(n) (cap)* (Christianity) The story of the birth of Jesus Christ

NATURE [Double R] [NA-RR-ATE]

> *(n)* Natural scenery;
> An unlearnt disposition

NATURAL [NAT-U-RAL] (adj) (v)

NAUSEATE [NAUS-E-ATE]

> *(v)* To make sick

NAUSEOUS [NAUS-E-OUS]

> *(adj)* Causing sickness

NAUGHT [NAU-GHT]

> *(adj)* Nothing
>
> e.g.: 'All for naught…'
>
> *or*

NOUGHT [NOU-GHT]

> *(adj)* Zero (0)

NAVIGATE [Middle I] [NAV-I-GATE]

> *(v)* To plan a route

~~naw~~ (bite) → GNAW

~~nay~~ (horse noise) → NEIGH

~~naybour~~ (next door) → NEIGHBOUR

~~naykid~~ (no clothes) → NAKED

~~naypalm~~ (incendiary) → NAPALM

Ne

NEANDERTHAL [NE-AN-DER-THAL]

(n) (cap) An extinct ancestor to humans

NECESSARILY [One C] [Double S] [NE-CESS-RA-ILY]

(adv) Unavoidable

NECESSARY [One C] [Double S] [NE-CESS-ARY]

(adj) Essential and needed

NECESSITATE [One C] [Double S] [NE-CESS-I-TATE]

(v) To make needed

NECESSITY [One C] [Double S] [NE-CESS-ITY]

(n) Something or someone that is essential

neche (specialised) → NICHE

NEED [N-EED]

Def 1: *(v)* To want something as it is essential

Def 2: *(n)* Something that is needed;
Being required to do something

or

KNEAD [K-NEAD]

(v) To work dough or clay;
To massage

NEGATIVE [One I] [NE-GA-TIVE]

Def 1: *(n)* Less than zero;
Showing absence of something

Def 2: *(v)* To be the opposite of positive;
To be gloomy or downbeat

NEGLECT [NE-GLECT]

Def 1: *(v)* To fail to give attention to

Def 2: *(n)* Being uncared for

NEIGH [NE-I-GH]

Def 1: *(n)* The sound a horse makes

Def 2: *(v)* To produce the sound a horse
makes

Ne

NEIGHBOUR [NEIGH-BOUR]

Def 1: *(n)* A person who lives next to your property

Def 2: *(v)* To be close to

Neighbor is US English only

NEMESIS [Middle E] [NEM-E-SIS]

(n) An archenemy;
The cause of someone's or something's downfall;
The Greek goddess of revenge

NEPHEW [No F] [NE-PH-EW

(n) The son of your brother or sister

nervana (peace) → NIRVANA

NERVOUS [NER-VO-US]

(n) Easily frightened;
Worried

nessecary (needed) → NAKED

nestalgia (memories) → NOSTALGIA

NEW [N-EW]

(n) Recently created, birth or made;
Not previously used or owned

or

KNEW [K-NEW]

(v) The past tense of to KNOW

newmonia (illness) → PNEUMONIA

newonce (slight difference) → NUANCE

Ni

NICHE [NI-CH-E]

> *(n)* Specialised and well fitting;
>   Not popular but still interests a small
>   selection of people;
>   A shallow recess within a wall

~~nieve~~ (innocence) → NAIVE

NIHILISM [NI-HIL-ISM]

> *(n)* The belief that nothing has value

~~nilon~~ (material) → NYLON

NIGHT [N-IGHT]

> *(n)* The period of time from sunset to sunrise

or

KNIGHT [K-NIGHT]

> Def 1: *(n)* A high ranking medieval fighter;
>   A sir;
>   A chess piece that moves in a 'L'
>   shape

NIRVANA [NIR-VANA]

(n) (Buddhism) A state of perfect inner peace

NIT [N-IT]

(n) The egg of a louse

vs

KNIT [Silent K] [K-NIT]

(v) To make by connecting yarn

No

NOCTURNAL [No K] [NOC-TURN-AL]

(adj) Activities done at night time

~~nock~~ (tap) → KNOCK

~~noll~~ (hill) → KNOLL

~~nome~~ (tiny being) → GNOME

NON [NON]

(Prefix) Meaning not

*Note: NON must be attached to
a separate word
(i.e.: NON-BELIEVER; NONSENSE)*

or

NONE [NON-E]

Def 1: *(pro)* Not any

Def 2: *(adj)* Not existing;
Not at all

NON SEQUITUR [Latin] [NON   SE-QUIT-ER]

(n) Not following on

No

~~noomatic~~ (machine) → PNEUMATIC

~~noomonia~~ (image) → PNEUMONIA

~~norseate~~ (sicken) → NAUSEATE

NOSTALGIA [NO-STAL-GIA]

(n) Looking back at the past with happiness

NOT [N-OT]

(n) Forbid;
  Negative

or

KNOT [K-NOT]

(n) A fastening;
  A tightening;
  A tangled mass;
  A hard mass within a tree;
  A maritime unit of speed

NOUGAT [Pronounced *noo-gat*] [NOU-GAT]

(adj) A type of sweet

No

NOUGHT [NOU-GHT]

(adj) Zero (0)

or

NAUGHT [NAU-GHT]

(adj) Nothing (e.g.: 'All for naught…')

NOW [N-OW]

(adv) Presently

or

KNOW [K-NOW]

(v) To be aware of;
To be certain

NOXIOUS [NOX-I-OUS]

(adj) Unpleasant

NUANCE [NU-ANCE]

(n) To be aware of;
To be certain

NUCLEAR [NU-CLEAR]

(n) Related to a nucleus;
Using energy creating by atomic fission or
fusion

NUCLEUS [NU-CLE-US]

(n) The core of an atom;
The part of a cell that controls its growth;
Central

~~nuematic~~ (machine) → PNEUMATIC

NUISANCE [NU-I-SANCE]

(n) Annoyance

NUMB [Ending with a silent B] [NU-MB]

Def 1: *(n)* Having no feeling

Def 2: *(v)* To cause to have no feeling

NURSERY [No A] NU-CLE-US]

(n) A place to tach and look after young
children;
A place to grow and sell plants

Ny

~~nyeve~~ (innocence) → NAIVE

NYLON [NY-LON]

(n) A synthetic fibre

NYMPH [No T] [NY-MPH]

(n) (folklore) A spirit from Greek and Roman
myths

~~nyooance~~ (slight difference) → NUANCE

O

Oa

OAK [O-AK]

(n) A large tree that produces acorns

OAR [O-AR]

(n) A paddle

vs

OR [O-R]

(conjunction) Giving a choice;
Rephrasing or alternative

OASIS [O-A-SIS]

(n) A fertile area within a desert;
A peaceful area

OATH [O-ATH]

(n) A vow or promise

Ob

OBEDIENT [OB-ED-ENT]

(adj) Follows instructions

OBESE [OB-ESE]

(adj) Extremely fat

OBJECT [No G] [OB-JECT]

(adj) A physical thing that can be interacted
with;
Something towards which thoughts,
feelings or actions are directed;
A goal

OBNOXIOUS [OB-NOX-IOUS]

(adj) Annoying

OBSCENE [OB-SCENE]

(adj) Sexual or disgusting;
A large amount

OBSTACLE [OB-S-TA-CLE]

(n) Something in the way

OBVIOUS [No E] [OB-VIOUS]

(adj) Being easily seen or found;
Predictable

OCARINA [OC-A-RIN-A]

(n) A wind instrument

OCCASION [Double C] [One S] [OC-CAS-ION]

(n) An event or moment in time

OCCULT [Double C] [OB-SCENE]

(n) Supernatural beliefs

OCCUPANT [Double C] [No E] [OC-CU-PANT]

(adj) A person occupying a place

OCCUPY [Double C] [OC-CU-PY]

(v) To take control of;
To fill;
To live or work in

OCCUR [Double C] [OC-CUR]

(v) To happen

Oc

OCHRE [Hidden H] [Ending -RE] [OC-H-RE]

(n) A yellowish-brownish colour

OCTAGON [No E] [OCT-A-GON]

(n) An eight-sided shape

OCTAVE [OC-TAVE]

(n) A series of eight musical notes

OCTOBER [OCT-O-BER]

(n) The 10th month of the year

Oe

OESOPHAGUS [Silent O] [O-ES-OPH-AGUS]

(n) The connection between the throat and the stomach

Esophagus is US English only

OESTROGEN [Silent O] [O-ESTRO-GEN]

(n) One of the female sex hormones

Estrogen is US English only

Of

OFFENCE [Double F] [OF-FENCE]

> *(n)* An illegal act;
> Hurt

OFFICIAL [Double F] [Two I's] [OFF-I-CIAL]

> *(adj)* Authorised

Og

OGRE [Ending -RE] [OG-RE]

> *(n) (folklore)* A man-eating giant

Oh

~~ohker~~ (colour) → OCHRE

~~ohnerous~~ (effort) → ONEROUS

~~ohnus~~ (responsibility) → ONUS

Ok

~~oke~~ (tree) → OAK

Ol

OLYMPIC [O-LYM-PIC]

> *(adj) (cap)* Relating to the Olympic games, an
> international sporting competition;
> Massive

Om

OMELETTE [Single M] [Double T] [OM-E-LE-TT-E]

(n) A type of food made from beaten eggs

On

~~oncore~~ (extra performance) → ENCORE

ONEROUS [ON-ER-OUS]

(adj) Required a lot of effort

ONION [No ending E] [ON-ION]

(n) A vegetable

~~ontreprenuar~~ (business) → ENTREPRENEUR

ONUS [O-NUS]

(n) Responsibility

ONYX [ON-YX]

(n) A semi-precious gem stone

Oo

OODLES [Double O] [OO-DLES]

> *(n) (pl) (informal)* Many

OOZE [Double O] [O-OZE]

> *(v)* To slowly seep out

Op

OPAL [No E] [O-PAL]

> *(n)* A semi-precious gem stone

OPALESCENT [OPAL-ES-CENT]

> *(adj)* Showing points of shifting colour

OPAQUE [OP-A-QUE]

> *(adj)* Cannot be seen through;
> Difficult to understand

Op

OPERA [OP-ERA]

(adj) A type of play set to music

OPERATE [OPER-ATE]

(v) To control;
To perform surgery

OPINION [O-PIN-ION]

(n) A personal viewpoint

OPPOSE [Double P] [OP-POSE]

(v) To disagree with

OPT [O-PT]

(v) To choose

OPTICIAN [One T] [OP-TIC-IAN]

(n) A maker or seller of visual aids

OPTION [OP-T-ION]

(n) A choice

OR [O-R]

(conjunction) Giving a choice;
Rephrasing or alternative

vs

OAR [O-AR]

(n) A paddle

ORCHESTRA [OR-CHEST-RA]

(n) A group of woodwind, brass, string and percussion musicians playing together in harmony

ORCHESTRATE [OR-CHEST-RATE]

(v) To arrange the score to an orchestral performance;
To plan, resulting in a desired result

Or

ORDINANCE [OR-DIN-ANCE]

(n) An official order

vs

ORDNANCE [No I] [ORD-NANCE]

(n) Larges guns or military equipment

OREGANO [Pronounced *O-RI-GAN-O*]
[OR-E-GAN-O]

(n) A type of herb

~~orfan~~ (deceased parents) → ORPHAN

ORGANISE [No middle E] [OR-GAN-ISE]

(v) To arrange

Also acceptable is ORGANIZE

ORNAMENT [No I] [ORN-A-MENT]

(n) A decorative item

ORPHAN [No F] [OR-PHAN]

(n) A person whose parents have died

~~orthentic~~ (real) → AUTHENTIC

OVERLEAF [OVER-LEAF]

(adv) On the other side of a page

OVERSTEER [Three E's] [OVER-STEER]

(v) To turn more sharply than intended

OWE [Ending E] [OW-E]

(v) To be required to pay or do something

OWL [OW-L]

(n) A large nocturnal bird of prey

Ox

OXYACETYLENE [OXY-ACE-TY-LENE]

(adj) A type of welding torch

OXYGEN [No I] [OX-Y-GEN]

(n) An elemental gas

| Chemical element symbol = **O** |
| Atomic number = **8** |

OXYMORON [No I] [OX-Y-MORON]

(n) A contradiction of terms or implications

Oy

OYSTER [No I] [OY-STER]

(n) An edible shellfish

P

PACHYDERM [Pronounced PACK-Y-DERM] [PACH-Y-DERM]

(n) Animals that are large and thick skinned
(e.g.: Elephants; Rhinoceroses; Hippopotamuses)

PACIFISM [No U] [PAC-I-FISM]

(n) A belief in not using violence

~~pactience~~ (waiting) → PATIENCE

PADRE [Spanish] [Ending -RE] [PAD-RE]

(n) A Chaplin

Translates to 'Father'

PAELLA [Spanish] [PA-ELLA]

(n) A Spanish dish with rice and seafood

PAGEANT [PAGE-ANT]

(n) A colourful ceremony

Pa

PAIL [P-AIL]

> *(n)* A bucket

vs

PALE [P-ALE]

> Def 1: *(adj)* Having little to no colour

> Def 2: *(v)* To have little to no colour

pajamas (Clothing) → PYJAMAS
(US English)

PALAEOLITHIC [PALA-EO-LITHIC]

> *(n)* Relating to the early stone-age era

PAPARAZZI [PAPA-RA-ZZI]

> *(n)* A group of photographers who follow celebrities

> *The singular is PAPARAZZO*

PAPAYA [PAP-AY-A]

> *(n)* A tropical fruit

~~paper-mache~~ (material) → PAPIER MÂCHÉ

PAPIER MÂCHÉ [French] [Not paper]
[PA-PIER MÂ-CHÉ]

(n) A material made from paper pulp

Translates to 'chewed paper'

PAPYRUS [Egyptian] [PAP-Y-RUS]

(n) Ancient Egyptian paper

PARACETAMOL [PARA-CET-A-MOL]

(n) A painkilling medicine

PARADISE [No -er] [PAR-A-DISE]

(n) Heaven;
A beautiful place

PARAGRAPH [Ending -PH] [PARA-GRAPH]

(n) A new, distinct line of writing

PARALLEL [Three L's] [PARA-LL-EL]

Def 1: *(adj)* Side by side;
Opposite

Def 2: *(n)* Similar;
A comparison

Pa

PARALLELOGRAM [Three L's]
[PARAL-LE-LO-GRAM]

(n) A quadrilateral shape with two pairs of parallel lines

PARALYMPICS [PAPA-LYMPICS]

(n) (cap) (pl) A sporting competition for those with disabilities

PARALYSE [PARA-LYSE]

(v) To make something or someone unable to move

Paralyze is US English only

PARAPLEGIA [No H] [PARA-PLE-GIA]

(n) Unable to move their legs

PARENTHESIS [No H] [PARENT-H-E-SIS]

(n) Added as an explanation

~~paraoh~~ (Egyptian ruler) → PHARAOH

PARROT [Double R] [PAR-ROT]

(n) A type of bird

Pa

PARTIAL [Ending -IAL] [PART-IAL]

(n) Not whole;
Bias

PARTICULAR [PART-IC-U-LAR]

Def 1: *(adj)* A member of a group;
Especially great

Def 2: *(n)* Details

~~parculiar~~ (dreams) → PECULIAR

~~pasificum~~ (peace) → PACIFISM

PASTRY [PA-STRY]

(n) A dough used for pies and other
desserts;
A type of cake

or

PASTY [No R] PA-STY]

(n) A folded pastry filled with meat and
vegetables (e.g.: Cornish Pasty)

PATIENCE [PA-TI-ENCE]

(n) The ability to wait without fuss;
A card game (also known as solitaire)

Pe

PEAL [P-EAL]

    Def 1: *(n)* A loud ringing noise

    Def 2: *(v)* To ring loudly

or

PEEL [Double E] [P-EEL]

    Def 1: *(v)* To remove the outer layer

    Def 2: *(n)* The outer skin of a fruit or vegetable

~~peasent~~ (bird) → PHEASANT

~~pease~~ (track) → PISTE

PEDAL [PED-AL]

    (n) A lever operated by foot

or

PEDDLE [Double D] [PED-D-LE]

    (v) To sell

~~peom~~ (writing) → POEM

~~penominal~~ (amazing) → PHENOMENAL

PENSION [No T] [PEN-SION]

(n) Money saved to be used in retirement

PENULTIMATE [PEN-ULT-I-MATE]

(adj) The last but one

PEPPERONI [PEPPER-ONI]

(n) A type of sausage chiefly used on pizzas

PERCUSSION [PER-CUSS-ION]

(n) A musical instrument where noise is made by banging or shaking

PERFORATED [PER-FOR-ATED]

(adj) Pierced

PERFUME [PER-FUME]

Def 1: *(n)* A nice scent

Def 2: *(v)* To make someone or something smell nice

Pe

PERHAPS [PER-HAPS]

(adv) Used to express uncertainty

PERIPHERY [No F] [PER-I-PH-ERY]

(n) On the outer edge

PERMANENT [PER-MA-NENT]

(n) Not leaving or being removed

~~persue~~ (chase) → PURSUE

PERSPECTIVE [PER-SPECT-IVE]

(n) Seeing something;
Relative to something else

PERSUADE [PER-SU-ADE]

(v) To convince

PERSUASIVE [PER-SU-A-SIVE]

(adj) Convincing

PHALANX [PHAL-AN-X]

> *(n)* A group of things or people

PHALLUS [Double L] [PH-ALL-US]

> *(n)* A penis

~~phantasise~~ (dreams) → FANTASISE

~~phantasy~~ (dreams) → FANTASY

PHARAOH [Egyptian] [PHA-RA-OH]

> *(n)* An ancient Egyptian ruler

PHARMACEUTICAL [PHARA-MA-CEU-TICAL]

> *(adj)* Relating to medicinal drugs

PHASE [PH-ASE]

> Def 1: *(n)* A stage in development
>
> Def 2: *(v)* To introduce gradually

vs

PHRASE [PH-R-ASE]

> *(n)* A saying

Ph

PHEASANT [Ending -ANT] [PHEA-SANT]

> (n) A game bird

PHENOMENAL [PHE-NOM-E-NAL]

> (adj) Brilliant

PHEROMONE [PHER-O-MON-E]

> (n) A chemical scent produced by animals

PHLEGM [Pronounced *flem]* [PH-LE-GM]

> (n) Mucus

PHLEGMATIC [PH-LEG-MATIC]

> (n) Calm and unemotional

PHOENIX [Hidden O] [PH-OE-NIX]

> (n) (folklore) A bird that ignites itself to be reborn from the ashes

PHONETIC [PHONE-TIC]

> (n) Representing sounds and speech

PHOTOGRAPH [PHOTO + GRAPH]

Def 1: *(n)* An image taken by a camera

Def 2: *(v)* To take an image

PHOTOSYNTHESIS [PHOTO-SYN-THE-SIS]

(n) The process by which plants use sunlight,
water and carbon dioxide to create
oxygen and energy

PHYSICAL [One l] [PHY-SI-CAL]

(adj) Can be touched;
Movement

PHYSIQUE [PHY-SI-QUE]

(n) The way a person body looks

Pi

PICCOLO [Double C] PIC-CO-LO]

(n) A small woodwind instrument

PICTURE [PIC-TURE]

Def 1: *(n)* An image, photograph or drawing

Def 2: *(v)* To take an image;
To imagine

PICTURESQUE [PIC-TURE-SQUE]

(adj) A charming location or building

PIEBALD [PIE-BALD]

(adj) (of a horse) Having two irregular colours

PIECE [PIC-TURE-SQUE]

Def 1: *(n)* Part of;
A work

Def 2: *(v)* To put together

PIÈCE DE RÉSISTANCE
[French] [PIÉ-CE DE RE-SIS-TANCE]

(n) The most impressive feature

PIER [PI-ER]

(n) A landing promenade for a ship or boat

PIERCE [PI-ER-CE]

(v) To make a hole

PIGEON [Starting PIG-] [PIG-EON]

(n) A type of bird

PILAF [One L] [PIL-AF]

(v) To steal (mainly small items or amounts)

PIOUS [PIG-OUS]

(adj) Deeply religious

PIP [P-IP]

Def 1: *(n)* A small seed;
A star on a officers uniform showing rank
Value indications on dice

Def 2: *(v)* To narrowly beat

PIPETTE [Double T] [PIP-ETTE]

(n) A device from transferring liquid

Pi

PIRANHA [One R] [PIR-AN-HA]

(n) A fish with sharp teeth

PISTE [French] [PI-STE]

(n) A ski slope or track

~~pithon~~ (snake) → PYTHON

PIVOT [No E] [PI-VOT]

(n) The point of which something moves

PLACEBO [Pronounced *plah-see-bo*]
[PLA-CE-BO]

(n) Something which gives the illusion of benefits despite having no effect

PLAGUE [Ending E] [PLAG-UE]

Def 1: *(n)* An infectious disease;
An infestation of insects

Def 2: *(v)* To cause trouble

PLAIN [P-LAIN]

(n) Simple;
Easy to see or understand;
Having no pattern

or

PLANE [P-LANE]

(n) Flat;
An aeroplane

PLAIT [Silent I] [P-LAIT]

(v) To weave hair or rope into a single strand

PLAQUE [No C] [No K] [PLA-QUE]

(n) A commentative sign on the wall;
Sticky deposits on teeth

PI

PLETHORA [PLETH-OR-A]

(n) A large quantity

PLIABLE [PL-I-ABLE[

(adj) Bendable

PLOUGH [P-LOUGH]

Def 1: *(n)* A machine for turning up ground

Def 2: *(v)* To turn soil for planting;
To carry on regardless of difficulty

Plow is US English only

PLUMB [Silent B] [PLUM-B]

Def 1: *(v)* To connect to water;
To test with a plumb line;

Def 2: *(n)* A weight connected to a line

PLUME [PLUM-E]

(n) A long feather;
Horse hairs producing from a helmet

Pn

PNEUMATIC [Silent P] [P-NEU-MATIC]

(adj) Containing or operated by gas under pressure

PNEUMONIA [Silent P] [P-NEU-MONIA]

(n) Inflammation of the lungs

~~pneumonic~~ (memory aid) → MNEMONIC

Po

POEM [PO-EM]

(n) A piece of writing

POIGNANT [POI-GN-ANT

(n) Bringing sadness and regret, or deep thoughts

POLITE [Ending -ET] [POL-ITE]

(adj) Respectful;
Civilised

POLTERGEIST [POLTER-GUIST]

(n) A ghost that physically interacts with objects

Po

POMEGRANATE [POM-E-GRAN-ATE]

(n) A tropical fruit

POMMEL [POM-MEL]

(n) Part of a saddle;
The end of a swords hilt

POPPY [PO-PP-Y]

(n) A plant

PORCELAIN [POR-CE-LAIN]

(n) Fine china

PORCUPINE [No K] [POR-CU-PINE]

(n) A spikey mammal

PORPOISE [POR-POISE]

(n) A small whale

PORTCULLIS [PORT-CULL-IS]

(n) A gate to a castle

POSTHUMOUS [No E] [POST-HUM-OUS]

(adj) occurring after death

POTATO [No E] [PO-TATO]

(n) A vegetable

POTENTIAL [PO-TEN-IAL]

Def 1: *(adj)* Capable of being

Def 2: *(n)* Qualities that may develop over time

~~potograph~~ (image) → PHOTOGRAPH

~~poyniant~~ (deep) → POIGNANT

Pr

PRACTICE [PRAC-TICE]

> *(v)* The application or use of an idea or method;
> The work of a doctor, dentist or lawyer;
> Repeatedly to improve a skill

vs

PRACTISE [PRAC-TISE]

> *(v)* To do repeatedly to improve a skill
> To do a certain job

Only in US English is the verb spelt *Practice*

PRECIOUS [PRE-CI-OUS]

(adj) Value or loved

PRECIPITATION [PRE-CIP-I-TATION]

(adj) Rain, sleet or snow

PRECISE [PRE-CI-SE]

(adj) Clear and unambiguous

PREFABRICATE [PRE-FAB-RI-CATE]

(adj) Building made in advance

PREDICAMENT [PRE-DIC-A-MENT]

(n) A difficult situation

PREGNANT [PREG-NANT]

(n) To have a child within the womb

~~prehaps~~ (maybe) → PERHAPS

PREJUDICE [PRE-JUDICE]

Def 1: *(v)* To judge based on preconceived notions, not evidence

Def 2: *(n)* A biased opinion based on pre-conceived notions

PRESSURE [Double S] [PRESS-URE]

(n) Steady force;
Stress

PRETZEL [No S] [PRET-ZEL]

(n) A knot shaped bread

PREVIOUS [PRE-VI-OUS]

(adj) Before

Pr

PRIMARY [PRIM-ARY]

> *(n)* First;
> Most important

PRINCE [PR-INCE]

> *(n)* The son or close family member of a ruler

PRINCESS [PR-INCE-SS]

> *(n)* The daughter or close family member of a ruler

PRINCIPAL [Ending -AL][PRIN-CI-PAL]

Def 1: *(adj)* The most important

Def 2: *(n)* The most important person;
The head teacher at a school or collage;
Relating to money lent or invested

or

PRINCIPLE [Ending -AL] [PRIN-CI-PLE]

> *(n)* A truth or believe that is used as a basis for something

---

PRIVILEGE [No D] [PRI-VIL-EGE]

> *(n)* A special right

PROBABLE [PRO-ABLE]

(adj) Likely

PROCURE [PRO-CURE]

(v) To acquire

PROGRAMME [PRO-CURE]

Def 1: *(n)* Television or radio;
Display to a potentially wide
audience;
A booklet with information about a
performance

Def 2: *(v)* To create a computer code;
To plan

PROHIBIT [PRO-HIB-IT]

(v) To ban

PROJECT [No G] [PRO-JECT]

Def 1: *(n)* Planned work
Research

Def 2: *(v)* To plan;
To estimate
To make an image show
To stick out

Pr

PROLIFERATE [PRO-LIFER-ATE]

(v) To reproduce quickly;
To grow quickly

PROMINENT [One E] [PRO-MIN-ENT]

(adj) Standing out

PRONOUNCE [PRO-NOU-CE]

(v) To say

PRONUNCIATION [PRO-NUN-CI-ATION]

(n) How words are said

PROPHECY [PRO-PH-ECY]

(n) A prediction

PROPHESY [PRO-PH-ESY]

(v) To make a prediction

PROSECUTE [PRO-SE-CUTE]

(v) To take legal action against

PROTEIN [PRO-TEIN]

(n) A molecule made up of amino acids

PROVOKE [PRO-VOKE]

(v) To cause a reaction

Ps

PSALM [Silent P] [P-SALM]

(n) A religious song or poem dedicated to God

PSEUDO [Silent P] [P-SEU-DO]

(adj) Fake

PSEUDONYM [Silent P] [P-SEU-DO-NYM]

(adj) A fake name

PSYCHIATRY [Silent P] [PSY-CHI-AT-RY]

(n) The study and management of mental illness

PSYCHIC [Silent P] [PSY-CH-IC]

Def 1: *(adj)* Mental abilities that cannot be explained by science

Def 2: *(n)* A person claiming to be physic

PSYCHOPATH [Silent P] [PSY-CHO-PATH]

(n) A person who feels no remorse or empathy

PSYCHOSOMATIC [Silent P] [PSYCHO-SO-MATIC]

(n) A physical illness symptoms caused by the mind

Pt

PTERODACTYL [Silent P]
[P-TER-O-DAC-TYL]

(n) A flying dinosaur

Pu

~~puhpyris~~ (Egyptian paper) → PAPYRUS

~~puhrentasis~~ (explanation) → PARENTHESIS

~~pumell~~ (saddle; sword) → POMMEL

~~purcussion~~ (drums) → POIGNANT

PURSUE [PUR-SUE]

(v) To chase or follow
To try to achieve

PYJAMAS [PY-JAMAS]

(n) (pl) Clothes for sleeping in

Pajamas is US English

PYTHON [PY-THON]

(n) A large snake

Q

Remember Q always needs to be followed by a U.

For example:

QUACK [QU-ACK]

QUADRANT [QUAD-RANT]

QUADRANT [QUAD-RANT]

QUALIFICATION [QUALI-FI-CATION]

QUALIFY [QUAL-I-FY]

QUANTITY [QUAN-TIT-Y]

QUEEN [QU-EEN]

QUICK [QU-ICK]

QUIRK [QU-IRK]

Qua

QUASAR [Pronounced *kway-sar*] [QUA-SAR]

(n) Galactic cores that emit massive amounts of electromagnetic radiation

QUAVER [QUA-VER]

Def 1: *(v)* To have a trembling voice

Def 2: *(n)* A shaky voice due to emotion; A musical note

Not to be confused with QUIVER

QUAY [Pronounced KEE] [QU-AY]

(n) A platform for loading and unloading ships

Que

QUELL [Pronounced KWELL] [QU-ELL]

(v) To suppress

QUERY [QU-ERY]

Def 1: *(v)* To question
To raise doubts

Def 2: *(n)* A question

Que

~~quesine~~ (food) → CUISINE

QUEUE [Ending -EU] QU-E-UE]

Def 1: *(v)* To wait in a line

Def 2: *(n)* A line of people waiting

Qui

QUICHE [Pronounced KEESH] [QU-I-CHE]

(n) An open pastry case filled with a savoury (non-sweet) filling

QUINTESSENCE [QUIN-TESS-ENCE]

(n) A perfect example

QUINTESSENTIAL [QUINT-ESS-EN-TIAL]

(adj) An example that represents something perfectly

QUIRK [QUI-RK]

(n) A habit not done by many people; An unusual occurrence

Qui

QUIVER [QUIV-ER]

Def 1: *(v)* To shake

Def 2: *(n)* A shaking movement
A case for keeping arrows in

Not to be confused with QUAVER

QUIZ [No S] [QU-IZ]

Def 1: *(v)* To test knowledge

Def 2: *(n)* A series of questions

Quo

QUORUM [QUOR-UM]

(n) The number of people needed to be valid

QUOTE [QU-OTE]

(v) To repeat someone's statement;
To give an estimated price

QUOTA [QU-OTA]

(n) The expected amount needed to be fulfilled

R

Ra

RABBI [Double B] [RAB-BI]

(n) A Jewish religious leader

RACCOON [Double C] [Double O] [RAC-COON]

(n) An American mammal with a black and white tail

RACQUET [RAC-QUET]

(n) A Paddle used in sports (e.g.: tennis; squash)

vs

RACKET [RAC-KET]

(n) A paddle used in sports (e.g.: tennis; squash);
A loud noise;
A commotion;
A fraudulent scheme

RACIAL [No E] [RAC-IAL]

(adj) Relating or being based on race

Ra

RADIANT [No E] [RAD-I-ANT]

Def 1: *(adj)* Glowing;
Showing good health

Def 2: *(n)* Heat transmitted by radiation

RADIATE [RAD-I-ATE]

(v) To emit energy;
To spread out

RAISIN [RAI-SIN]

(n) A dried grape

RASPBERRY [Hidden P] [RAS-P-BERRY]

(n) A reddish vegetable

RASTAFARIAN [RASTA-FAR-IAN]

(n) A Jamaican religious movement

RATATOUILLE [One O] [Hidden U]
[RATA-TOU-ILLE]

(n) A French dish

RATIONAL [RATION-AL]

>   *(adj)* Logical

vs

RATIONALE [Ending E] [RATION-AL-E]

>   *(v)* Reasons for a believe

RAVIOLI [Two I's] [RAVI-OLI]

>   *(n)* A pasta dish

~~rawal~~ (country) → RURAL

~~rayson~~ (food) → RAISIN

Re

READ [RE-AD]

> *(v)* To understand written text;
> To speak written words out loud;
> To interpret

or

REED [RE-ED]

> *(n)* A marshy plant;
> A mouthpiece for some woodwind
> instruments

READY [Middle A] [RE-AD-Y]

(adj) Prepared and available

REAGENT [Middle A] [RE-A-GENT]

> *(n)* A substance or compound that can
> facilitate a reaction

vs

REGENT [RE-GENT]

Def 1: *(n)* A person appointed to act on the
monarchs behalf if they are under
the age of 18 or they become
permanently incapacitated due to
"infirmity of mind or body"

Def 2: *(adj)* Acting as a regent

REALIGN [One L] [RE-AL-IGN]

(v) To change position

REALISE [REAL-ISE]

(v) To become aware of;
To achieve
Realize is US English only

REALM [Middle A] [RE-A-LM]

(n) A kingdom;
An area of interest

REALLY [Double L] [RE-ALL-Y]

(adv) In reality

REASSURE [Double S] [RE-ASS-URE]

(v) To make feel better

RECCE [Double C] [No K]] [RE-CC-E]

(n) Short for reconnaissance

Re

RECEIPT [Middle I] [RE-CE-I-PT]

(n) Evident something has been received

~~recent~~ (bitterness) → RESENT

RECOGNISE [RE-COG-NISE]

(v) To identify;
To accept the legitimacy of

Recognize is US English only

RECOMMEND [Double M] [REC-O-MM-END]

(v) To suggest

RECONNAISSANCE [RE-CONN-AI-SS-ANCE]

(n) Observation to gather intelligence

RECREATE [RE-CREATE]

(v) To do again

RECRUIT [RE-CRUIT]

Def 1: *(v)* To employ someone

Def 2: *(n)* A new person

RECTANGLE [Middle T] [REC-TANGLE]

(v) A shape with 4 sides
(with at least two being unequal)

RECTIFY [RE-CT-IFY]

(v) To fix;
To convert alternate current into direct
current

RECYCLE [RE-CYCLE]

(v) To use unwanted items again in a new
form

REDEEM [RE-DEEM]

(v) To make up for faults or sins;
To exchange

REED [RE-ED]

(n) A marshy plant;
A mouthpiece for some woodwind
instruments

or

READ [RE-AD]

(v) To understand written text;
To speak written words out loud;
To interpret

Re

reenforce (support) → REINFORCE

REFER [No U] [RE-FER]

(n) To mention;
To be passed on to

REFEREE [Four E's] [REF-ER-EE]

Def 1: *(v)* To supervise to ensure rules are
followed

Def 2: *(n)* A person appointed to ensure rules
are followed

REFERENCE [One F] [REFER-ENCE]

(n) Acknowledging using other sources;
The action of mentioning something

REFERENDUM [REF-ER-EN-DUM]

(n) A vote on a singular issue

REFRIGERATOR [No D] [RE-FRIG-ER-ATOR]

(n) An appliance used for chilling food

REGALIA [RE-GAL-IA]

(n) The set of emblems, symbols and objects
signifying royal status

REGGAE [RE-GG-AE]

> *(n)* A Jamaican music style

REGIME [RE-GI-ME]

> *(n)* An ordered way of doing something;
> A government

REGISTER [No A] [RE-GIS-TER]

Def 1: *(n)* A list

Def 2: *(v)* To be placed on a register;
To express opinion

REGISTRAR [RE-GIST-RAR]

> *(n)* A senior doctor;
> A person responsible for maintaining
> records

REIGN [RE-IGN]

Def 1: *(v)* To rule

Def 2: *(n)* The years of a monarch's rule

vs

REIN [RE-IN]

> *(n)* Staps attached to a bit to control a horse

Re

REINFORCE [Middle -in-][RE-IN-FORCE]

(v) To strengthen and support

REJUVENATE [RE-JUV-EN-ATE]

(n) To give more energy or youth

RELEGATE [One L] [RE-LE-GATE]

(n) To demote

RELIEF [RE-LIEF]

(n) Relaxation after panic or hurt;
A carving
A person who replaces another

RELIEVE [RE-LIEVE]

(v) To reduce or remove panic or pain
To take over from someone;
To provide support from a military assault

RELIGION [RE-LI-GION]

(v) The belief and worship of a God or gods

RELIGIOUS [RE-LI-GI-OUS]

(adj) Belief in a religion;
To do regularly without fail

RELINQUISH [RE-LIN-QUISH]

(v) To give up

REMEMBER [REM-EM-BER]

(v) To recollect memories

REMINISCENT [REM-IN-I-SCENT]

(adj) When one thing reminds you of another

REMOTE [Ending E] RE-MOT-E]

(n) Far away;
    Unfriendly;
    A device used to control things

RENAISSANCE [French] RE-NAI-SS-ANCE]

(n) A revival in interest
(cap) The revival of classical art that took
    place in Italy around 1400 AD

RENDEZVOUS [French] [Middle Z] [REN-DEZ-VOUS]

(n) A time and a date to meet

RENEGE [No I] [RE-NE-GE]

(v) To fail to keep a promise

Re

REPAIR [RE-PAIR]

Def 1: *(v)* To fix

Def 2: *(n)* The act of fixing

REPOSSESS [RE-PO-SS-ESS]

(v) To take back when payment in not made

REQUIRE [RE-QU-IRE]

(v) To need;
To be ordered to do

RESENT [RE-SENT]

(v) To feel angry about

RESIGN [RE-SIGN]

(v) To voluntarily quit

RESPONSE [No C] [RE-SPON-SE]

(n) An answer or reaction

RESPONSIBILITY [RE-SPONS-I-BIL-ITY]

(n) To oversee

RESTAURANT [RE-STA-UR-ANT]

> *(n)* A place where food is cooked and served in exchange for money

REVEILLE [RE-VEI-LLE]

> *(n)* A time to wake up at, traditionally by a bugle

REVIEW [RE-VEIW]

> Def 1: *(v)* To critically analyse
>
> Def 2: *(n)* Checking for errors
> A critical analysis

REVOLVE [RE-VOL-VE]

> *(v)* To move around a central point

Rh

RHAPSODY [R-HAP-SODY]

(n) An emotional work of joy;
A piece of music with no formal structure

RHETORICAL [Hidden H] [RHE-TOR-I-CAL]

(adj) Not intended to be answered

RHINOCEROS [RHINO-CER-OUS]

(n) A large and powerful mammal

RHODODENDRON [RHODO-DEN-DREN]

(n) A type of plant

RHOMBUS [Hidden H] [RHOM-BUS]

(n) A shape that has four equally long sides

RHUBARB [Hidden H] [RHU-BARB]

(n) A plant with edible red stalks

RHYME [Hidden H] [RH-Y-ME]

Def 1: *(n)* Words ending in similar sounds

Def 2: *(v)* To end a sentence with similar sounds

RHYTHM (n)

RICOCHET [No K] [RICO-CHET]

Def 1: *(n)* A shot that bounces off an object

Def 2: *(v)* To rebound

~~rigent~~ (caretaker) → REGENT

RIGHT [R-IGHT]

Def 1: *(adj)* Morally correct;
On the east side, opposite to left

Def 2: *(adv)* Correctly

Def 3: *(v)* To correct

Def 4: *(n)* An entitlement

vs

WRITE [WR-ITE]

(v) To mark out letters

RIGHTEOUS [RIGHT-E-OUS]

(adj) Ethically right

~~rime~~ (poetry) → RHYME

Ri

RINSE [No C] [RIN-SE]

Def 1: *(v)* To put water over a surface

Def 2: *(n)* The act of rinsing

RISQUÉ [French] [RIS-QUÉ]

(adj) Slightly naughty

~~rivalle~~ (wake up) → REVEILLE

~~rombus~~ (shape) → RHOMBUS

ROOK [R-OOK]

>*(n)* A type of bird related to the crow;
>>A chess piece that moves vertically or
>>horizontally

ROOKIE [No Y] [ROOK-IE]

>*(n) (informal)* A new, inexperienced person

ROSARY [No E] [RO-SA-RY]

>*(n)* A Catholic string of beads used to keep
>>count of prayers

~~roseydendrum~~ (plant) → RHODODENDRON

ROUGH [No F] [ROU-GH]

>*(n)* Harsh;
>>Not gentle

Ru

~~rubarb~~ (plant) → RHUBARB

RUMOUR [RU-MOUR]

(n) Gossip;
News that is not confirmed

Rumor is US English only

RURAL [RUR-AL]

(adj) The countryside

S

Sa

SABBATH [Double B] [No E] [SAB-BATH]

(n) A religious day of rest

SABOTAGE [No- U] [SAB-O-TAGE]

Def 1: *(v)* To destroy

Def 2: *(n)* The act of destroying

SABOTEUR [SAB-OT-EUR]

(n) A person who sabotages

SABRE [Ending -RE] [SAB-RE]

(n) A curved sword

Saber is US English only

SACRIFICE [SAC-RI-FICE]

Def 1: *(v)* To up something for a cause

Def 2: *(n)* The thing being given up

SADDLE [Double D] [Ending -LE] [SAD-DLE]

(n) A seat for sitting on a horse or bicycle

Sa

SAFARI [SAF-ARI]

(n) A trip to see animals in their natural environment

SAKE [SA-KE]

(n) For the purpose of

is spelt the same as

SAKE [Pronounced *SA-KI*] [SA-KE]

(n) A Japanese alcoholic rice drink

SALIVA [SA-LIV-A]

(n) Liquid created in the mouth

~~salm~~ (religious words) → PSALM

SAMARITAN [SA-MAR-I-TAN]

(n) (cap) A kind, selfless person

SAMURAI [Japanese] [SAM-U-RAI]

(n) A Japanese member of a high social rank from the 11th to the 19th century

SANDWICH [ONE H] [No T] [SAND-WI-CH]

Def 1: *(n)* Two pieces of bread surrounding a filling

Def 2: *(v)* To place in the middle of two objects

SANITISE [SAN-I-TISE]

(v) To make clean

Sanitize is US English

~~sany~~ (wacky) → ZANY

SAPPHIRE [No F] [Double P] [SA-PP-HIRE]

(n) A blue precious gemstone;
A blue colour

~~sar~~ (Russian Emperor) → TSAR

SARCASM [SAR-CAS-M]

(n) Remarks that mean the opposite of what they say

SARCOPHAGUS [SAR-CO-PH-A-GUS]

(n) A rock or stone coffin

Sa

SATELLITE [Double L] [SAT-E-LL-ITE]

Def 1: *(n)* An object, natural or man-made, that is in orbit around a planet

Def 2: *(adj)* A dependant

SAVOUR [SAV-OUR]

(v) To enjoy over a prolonged period

~~sayonce~~ (contacting the dead) → SEANCE

SCABBARD [Double B] [SCAB-BARD]

(n) A holder for a sword or knife

SCALENE [SCA-LENE]

(n) A triangle with unequal sides

SCAMPI [No Y] [SCAM-PI]

(v) A type of food made from breaded prawn tails

SCANDINAVIAN [SCAN-DI-NA-VIAN]

(adj) (cap) Relating to Nordic counties, but mainly Norway, Denmark and Sweden

SCARLET [SCAR-LET]

(n) A red colour

SCENARIO [SCEN-AR-IO]

(n) What may possibly happen

SCENE [SCE-NE]

(n) The place where something occurs; A continuous sequence in a play or film

Sc

SCEPTICAL [SCEP-TIC-AL]

(adj) Not convinced

SCEPTRE [SCEP-TRE]

(adj) A staff carried by a monarch

~~scewer~~ (stab) → SKEWER

SCHADENFREUDE [German]
[SCHADEN-FREUDE]

(n) Joy brought from other peoples misfortune

SCHEDULE [Ending E] [SCH-ED-ULE]

Def 1: *(n)* A guide to what is to occur

Def 2: *(v)* To plan for a set time

SCHEMATIC [SCH-E-MATIC]

(n) Outlining the main feature of something

SCHEME [SCH-EME]

Def 1: *(n)* A plan or plot

Def 2: *(v)* To plan

SCHISM [SCH-ISM]

> *(n)* A disagreement that causes people to split into groups

SCHIZOPHRENIA [SCH-IZO-PHR-ENIA]

> *(n)* A mental disorder

SCHOLAR [SCH-O-LAR]

> *(n)* A person being taught;
> A person studying at an advanced level

SCIENCE [SC-IE-N-CE]

> *(n)* The study or knowledge of the physical world

SCIENTIST (n)

SCHOOL [Middle H] [SC-H-OOL]

> *(n)* A place where people go to learn

SCIMITAR [Hidden C] [SCIM-I-TAR]

> *(n)* A type of sword;
> A type of tank

SCISSORS [Hidden C] [SC-ISS-ORS]

> *(n)* A cutting tool

Sc

SCLEROSIS [Hidden C] [SCIM-I-TAR]

(n) Abnormal Harding of bodily tissue;
An abnormally curved spined

MULTIPLE SCLEROSIS

SCRAWL [Hidden W] [SC-RA-WL]

(v) To write hurriedly

~~scumptuous~~ (lavish) → SUMPTUOUS

SEANCE [Hidden E] [SEA-NCE]

(n) Where people try to contact the dead

SEASON [SEA-SON]

Def 1: *(n)* One of the quarters of the year
(spring; summer; autumn; winter);
A time where certain weather is
dominant

Def 2: *(v)* To add to food for flavouring;
To dry wood

SECRET [Hidden C] [SC-ISS-ORS]

Def 1: *(adj)* To keep from others

Def 2: *(n)* Something kept from others

or

SECRETE [Ending E] [SE-CRET-E]

(v) To produce as substance;
To hide

~~seek~~ (religion) → SIKH

SEEMINGLY [SEEM-ING-LY]

(n) Appearing to be so but not confirmed

Se

~~segway~~ (uninterrupted join) → SEGUE

SEIZE [E before I] [SEI-ZE]

    (v) To take by force

    SEIZURE (n)

~~selcius~~ (temperature) → CELSIUS

~~sellebrate~~ (praise) → CELEBRATE

SEMINAR [Ending -AR] [SEM-IN-AR]

    (n) An educational meeting or presentation

~~senaligans~~ (tricks) → SHENANIGANS

SENTENCE [Double N] [SEN-TEN-CE]

    (n) A group of words that mean something;
    A punishment

SEPARATE [Middle -AR-] [SEP-AR-ATE]

    Def 1: *(n)* Individual

    Def 2: *(v)* To split and move apart

SEQUEL [No C] [No A] [SC-QU-EL]

    (n) Continuing on from a previous story

Se

SEQUENCE [One C] [SE-QU-EN-CE]

(n) The order in which things are performed

SERENADE [SE-REN-ADE]

(v) To play music to attract a partner

SERENDIPITY [SE-REN-DIP-ITY]

(n) Good luck in finding things

SERENE [SE-REN-E]

(adj) Peaceful

SERIAL [SE-RIAL]

Def 1: *(adj)* Repeating
Taking part in a series

Def 2: *(n)* Media that occurs over multiple
slots

vs

CEREAL [CE-REAL]

(n) A food eaten at breakfast;
A grain used for food

~~serink~~ (make smaller) → SHRINK

Se

SERMON [SER-MON]

> *(n)* A religious lecture

SERVANT [No F] [SER-VANT]

> *(n)* An employee who performs domestic work

~~serzairum~~ (birth) → CAESAREAN

SESSION [SE-SS-ION]

> *(n)* A period of time dedicated to something

~~sest~~ (skin; energy) → ZEST

SEVER [SEV-ER]

> *(v)* To cut off completely

SEVERE [Ending E] [SER-VR-E]

> *(n)* Time devoted to something

SEVEN [NO R] [SER-VER-E]

> *(n)* A number between 6 and 8 (7)

SEW [S-EW]

> *(v)* To join together using a needle and thread

vs

SOW [Pronounced *SO*] [S-OW]

> *(v)* To plant seeds

which is spelt the same as

SOW [Pronounced *SOWE*] [S-OW]

> *(n)* A female pig

Sh

~~shatoe~~ (French house) → CHATEAU

SHEATHE [Ending E] [SH-EA-TH-E]

(n) A cover for a sword or knife

SHEIKH [SH-EI-KH]

(n) An Arab leader

SHELF [SH-ELF]

(n) A flat surface

SHELVE [No F] [SH-EL-VE]

(v) To put on a shelf;
To stop work on

SHENANIGANS [SHEN-AN-I-GANS]

(n) (informal) A devious trick

SHEPHARD [Middle H] [SHEP-HARD]

(n) A person who looks after sheep

SHERIFF [Double F] [SHER-FF]

(n) An officer in charge of maintaining law
and order

SHAWL [Hidden W] [SH-A-WL]

(n) A piece of fabric that can be wrapped
around the body

Sh

SHEILD [E before I] [SH-EI-LD]

Def 1: *(v)* To defend

Def 2: *(n)* An object used to defend oneself

~~shiverouse~~ (polite) → CHIVALROUS

~~shivurhry~~ (medieval code) → CHIVALRY

~~shoffeur~~ (driver) → CHAUFFEUR

SHORE [SH-ORE]

(n) The land at the end of the sea

SHOULD [SH-OULD]

(mv) To express a wish;
A polite way of asking or ordering

SHOULDER [SH-OUL-DER] [SC-RA-WL]

Def 1: *(n)* The joint between the torso and arm

Def 2: *(v)* To take a burden

SHRINK [Hidden H] [SH-RINK]

(v) To make smaller

Si

SIAMESE CAT [SIAM-ESE CAT]

> *(n)* A type of cat from Siam (now Thailand)

~~siance~~ (study) → SCIENCE

SIESTA [Spanish] [SIE-STA]

> *(n)* An afternoon nap

SIEVE [SI-EVE]

> Def 1: *(n)* A mesh used to separate solids and liquids
>
> Def 2: *(v)* To put into a sieve

~~sifalis~~ (disease) → SYPHILIS

SIGH [SI-GH]

> *(v)* To let out a long breath

SIGN [SI-GN]

> Def 1: *(n)* Something giving direction
>
> Def 2: *(v)* To put a signature to

SIGNATURE [SIG-NAT-URE]

(n) A personalised way of wring your name;
Something only done by someone or
something

SIGNIFICANCE [SIG-IF-I-CANCE]

(n) Having an important meaning

SIGNIFY [SIG-NI-FY]

(v) To mean

SIKH [Pronounced *seek*] [S-I-K-H]

(n) A follower of Sikhism

~~silch~~ (nothing) → ZILCH

SILENCE [SI-LEN-CE]

(n) No noise generated or made

SILHOUETTE [SIL-HOU-ETTE]

(n) A dark shadow against a lighter
background

SILO [One L] [SI-LO]

(n) A tower for storing grain;
An underground tube for firing missiles

~~simbal~~ (percussion instrument) → CYMBAL

Si

SIMILAR [SIM-I-LAR]

> *(adj)* Like but not identical to

SIMILE [Pronounced SIM-I-LEE] [SIM-ILE]

> *(n)* A phrase that compares but is not literal, using like or as

~~simingly~~ (appearing) → SEEMINGLY

~~simitar~~ (sword; tank) → SCIMITAR

Be careful of '*sim*' sounding words as they may start with SY. For example:

~~simathry~~ (parallel) → SYMMETRY

~~simble~~ (feel sorry) → SYMBOL

~~simonym~~ (similar word) → SYNONYM

~~simpathetic~~ (feel sorry) → SYMPATHETIC

~~sinagog~~ (Jewish temple) → SYNAGOGUE

~~sindicate~~ (group) → SYNDICATE

~~sindrome~~ (symptoms) → SYNDROME

SIMPLIFY [SIMP-LI-FY]

(v) To make easier

SINCERE [Pronounced SIN-CER-E]
[SIN-CER-E]

(adj) Genuine

SIPHON [No F] [SI-PHON]

Def 1: *(n)* A tube used to move liquid via gravity

Def 2: *(v)* To take

vs

CIPHER [CI-PH-ER]

(n) A code

CYPHER is also acceptable

SIR [S-IR]

(n) A polite form of address to a male;
The title of a knight

or

SIRE [S-IR-E]

Def 1: *(v)* To father an animal

Def 2: *(n)* The father of an animal;
An old-fashioned way of
addressing king

Si

SIREN [No W] [SIR-EN]

> *(n)* A device that makes a loud noise

~~siringe~~ (injection device) → SYRINGE

SIRLOIN [SIR + LOIN]

> *(n)* A piece of beef which is cut from the
> bottom and side parts of a cows back

~~sirnk~~ (make smaller) → SHRINK

~~sissors~~ (cutting device) → SCISSORS

~~sirzareaum~~ (birth) → CAESAREAN

SITUATION [SITU-A-TION]

> *(n)* A set of circumstances

~~skisum~~ (disagreement) → SCHISM

SKELETON [No -ing-] [SK-EL-E-TON]

Def 1: *(n)* A supporting structure
The boney framework inside a body

Def 2: *(adj)* The smallest possible amount

~~skepical~~ (doubt) → SCEPTICAL

SKEWER [No -qu-] [SK-EW-ER]

Def 1: *(n)* A long stick used for holding pieces
of food while cooking

Def 2: *(adj)* To stab through

SKILFUL [No Double L's] [SKIL-FUL]

(n) Having or showing expertise

Skillfull is US English Only

SI

SLAVE [No F] [SL-A-VE]

Def 1: *(n)* A person owned by another

Def 2: *(v)* To work hard

SLAY [SL-AY]

(v) To kill

vs

SLEIGH [SLE-I-GH]

(n) A sledge (a land vehicle that slides across a surface, usually of ice or snow) drawn by horses or reindeer

---

SLEIGHT [Middle E] [SL-E-IGHT]

(n) Being able to use your hands with ease

vs

SLIGHT [S-LIGHT]

Def 1: *(adj)* A small amount

Def 2: *(n)* An insult

Def 3: *(v)* To insult

Sm

SMOULDER [SM-OU-LDER]

> *(v)* To burn without a flame;
> To barely hide anger

SMUGGLE [Ending -LE] [Double G] [SMUG-G-LE]

> *(v)* To move out secretly

Sn

~~senaligans~~ (tricks) → SHENANIGANS

SNORKEL [SNO-RK-EL]

> *(n)* A tube for breathing underwater

So

SOCIAL [Ending -IAL]

> *(n)* Relating to the company of others

SOCIETY [SOC-IE-TY]

> *(n)* People living together in communities

SOFTEN [Hidden T] [SOFT-EN]

> *(v)* To make softer

SOLDIER [SOL-DIER]

> *(n)* A person serving in the armed forces

So

SOLE [SO-LE]

Def 1: *(n)* The bottom of a foot or show

Def 2: *(adj)* The only one

vs

SOUL [SO-UL]

(n) A living creatures spirit;
A type of music

SOLICITOR [SOL-IC-ITOR]

(n) A lawyer

SOLITAIRE [SOL-IT-AIR-E]

(n) A one-person card game
(also called Patience);
A single gem within jewellery

SOLILOQUY [SOL-IL-O-QUY]

(n) A speech made by a character for the audience

SOMBRE [Ending -ER] [SOMBRE]

(n) A gloomy mood

Somber is US English Only

SOMBRERO [SOM-BRE-E-RO]

(n) A Mexican hat

SOMERSAULT [SOMER-SAULT]

(n) A movement in gymnastics

SOOTHE [Ending with an E] [Double O] [S-OO-TH-E]

(v) To calm/ remove pain and anxiety

SOOTHSAYER [No E] [SOOTH-SAYER]

(n) A prophet

SOPHISTICATED [SO-PHIS-TI-CATED]

(n) Complex;
Having knowledge of culture

SOPHOMORE [SO-PHO-MORE]

(n) A 2nd year student in the United States

SORBET [Pronounced *SOR-BAY*] [SOR-BET]

(n) A frozen dessert made using ice

SORCERER [SOR-CER-ER]

(n) A person who uses magic

So

SOUFFLÉ [French] [SOU-FF-LÉ]

(n) A light, airy desert

SOUL [SO-UL]

(n) A living creatures spirit;
A type of music

vs

SOLE [SO-LE]

Def 1: *(n)* The bottom of a foot or show

Def 2: *(adj)* The only one

~~sould~~ (request to do) → SHOULD

SOVEREIGN [SOV-E-REIGN]

Def 1: *(n)* To have absolute power

Def 2: *(adj)* A king or queen

SOVEREIGNTY [SOVE-REIGN-TY]

(n) Supreme power and independence

SOW [Pronounced *SO*] [S-OW]

(v) To plant seeds

which is spelt the same as

SOW [Pronounced *sowe*] [S-OW]

(n) A female pig

vs

SEW [S-EW]

(v) To join together using a needle and thread

Sp

SPECIAL [SPEC-IAL]

(n) Better or Different;
For a set purpose

SPECIFIC [SPEC-IF-IC]

(n) Defined

SPECIMEN [SPEC-I-MEN]

(n) An example

SPECTRE [Ending -RE] [SPEC-TRE]

(n) A ghost

Specter is US English Only

SPECTRUM [SPEC-TRUM]

(n) A range

~~speel~~ (speech) → SPIEL

SPELL [SP-ELL]

Def 1: *(v)* To write or say letters to form a
word

Def 2: *(n)* A short period of time;
Words to cast magic

SPHERE [No F] [SPH-ERE]

(n) A round, solid 3D-shape

SPHINX [SPH-INX]

(n) An ancient Egyptian symbol with a lions body and a human head

SPIEL [SP-I-EL]

(n) A speech that's intended to persuade or make excuses

SPIRIT [SP-I-RIT]

(n) Character;
A ghost;
A strong alcohol

SPLENDOUR [SP-LEN-DO-UR]

(n) Impressive appearance

Splendor is US English only

SPONSOR [No E] [SPON-SOR]

(n) A person or origination that gives money to something

Sp

SPREAD [No A] [SP-RE-AD]

(v) To extend over a larger area ·

SPREE [SP-REE]

(n) A period of doing an activity more than usual

Sq

SQUANDER [SQU-AN-DER]

(v) To waste

SQUAWK [No R] [SQU-AWK]

(n) A loud noise

~~squewer~~ (stab) → SKEWER

SQUIRREL [Double R] [Single L] [SQU-IRR-EL]

(n) A rodent with a large, bushy tail

Sr

~~srink~~ (make smaller) → SHRINK

STABILISE [STAB-IL-ISE]

(v) To make steady

Stabilize is US English Only

STALACTITE [Middle C] [STALA-C-TITE]

(n) Calium salt deposits forming from the roof of a cave

vs

STALAGMITE [STA-LAGMITE]

(n) Calium salt deposits forming from the floor of a cave

STAMPEDE [STAMP-EDE]

Def 1: *(n)* A sudden rush

Def 2: *(v)* To be in a large rushing group

STANDARD [STAND-ARD]

Def 1: *(n)* The required qualities needed;
A flag used in battle to organise troops

Def 2: *(adj)* Average

St

STAPLE [Ending -LE] [STAP-LE]

Def 1: *(n)* A joining metal clip for documents; Main

Def 2: *(v)* To join together

STARRIER [STAR-R-IER]

(adj) Having more stars than another thing

STASIS [No Y] [STA-SIS]

(n) Having no change

STATIONARY [Ending -ARY] [STA-TION-ARY]

(adj) Not moving

or

STATIONERY [Ending -ERY] [STA-TION-ERY]

(n) Writing materials

STEREO [Hidden E] [STER-EO]

(n) A type of sound; A CD player

STEREOTYPE [STEREO+TYPE]

(n) A widely held but oversimplified image

STERILE [STER-ILE]

(n) Unable to reproduce;
Free from bacteria or contamination

STIGMATISE [STIGMA-TISE]

(v) To reject due to being shameful

STILE [No Y] [ST-ILE]

(n) A stepping platform for crossing a fence
or wall

STOMACH [STOM-ACH]

(n) An organ for breaking down food

STOPPAGE [Double P] [STOP-PAGE]

(n) A blockage or cut supply that stops
movement

STOREY [Middle E] [STOR-EY]

(n) A level of a building

Story in terms of a building is US English only

vs

STORY [STOR-Y]

(n) A tale told to others

St

STRAIGHT [STR-IA-GHT]

(adj) To carry on without diverting;
Being level and having no bends;
Undiluted

STRAIT [STR-AIT]

(n) A narrow bod of water between two seas

STRAITS [Ending S] [STR-AIT-S]

(n) A bad situation

STRAITJACKET [No GH] [STRAIT + JACKET]

(n) A jacket with limited arm movement

STRUCTURE [STR-UCT-URE]

Def 1: (n) They was something is organised;
The main frame of a building

Def 2: (v) To organise

STRUDEL [German] [Ending -EL] [ST-RU-DEL]

(n) A type of pastry

~~stumach~~ (organ) → STOMACH

STYPTIC [No middle I] [ST-Y-PIC]

(adj) Something that is able to stop bleeding

SUBSIDISE [No A] [SUB-SID-ISE]

(v) To pay part of the cost

Subsidize is US English Only

SUBSTANTIAL [SUB-STAN-TIAL]

(adj) Important;
Large

SUBTLE [Silent B] [Ending -LE] [SUB-TLE]

(n) Movement or change so fine it can
barely be noticed;
Delicate

~~suffercate~~ (strangle) → SUFFOCATE

Be careful of silent P's. For example:

~~suedo~~ (fake) → PSEUDO

~~suedonym~~ (fake name) → PSEUDO

~~sychatry~~ (mental illness) → PSYCHIATRY

~~sycopath~~ (no empathy) → PSYCHOPATH

~~sykick~~ (mental abilities) → PSYCHIC

Su

SUGGEST [Double G] [SU-GG-EST]

(n) To mention an idea for consideration

SUMMARY [No E] [Double M] [SUM-MARY]

(n) A condensed version

SUMPTUOUS [No C] [SUMP-TU-OUS]

(n) Splendid and expensive looking

SUPERSEDE [No C] [SUPER-SEDE]

(v) To take over

SUPPRESS [Double P] [SUP-PRESS]

(v) To end with force or power

SURVIVE [Two V's] [SUR-VIV-E]

(v) To continue living

 (barely noticeable) → SUBTLE

Sw

SWEDE [SWE-DE]

(n) A root vegetable
(cap) (informal) A Swedish person

~~sychatry~~ (mental illness) → PSYCHIATRY

~~sycopath~~ (no empathy) → PSYCHOPATH

~~sykick~~ (mental abilities) → PSYCHIC

SYMBOL [No E] [Ending -BOL] [SYM-BOL]

> *(n)* A mark or character;
> A substitute for another meaning

~~symbal~~ (percussion instrument) → CYMBAL

SYMBOLISE [SYM-BOL-ISE]

> *(v)* To be a symbol

> *Symbolize* is US English Only

SYMMETRY [Double M] [SYM-MET-RY]

> *(n)* Being equal in movement

SYMPATHETIC [SYM-PATHETIC]

> *(adj)* Feeling sorry for

SYMPATHIZE [SYM-PATH-IZE]

> *(v)* To empathise and feel sorry for

SYMPTOM [Hidden middle P] [SYM-P-TOM]

> *(n)* A sign of something undesirable

Sy

SYNAGOGUE [SYNA-GOG-UE]

(n) A Jewish religious building

SYNCHRONISE [SYNCH-RO-NISE]

(v) To occur at the same time

Synchronize is US English only

SYNDICATE [SYN-DI-CATE]

Def 1: *(n)* A group of people with a common interest

Def 2: *(v)* To publish at the same time

SYNDROME [One N] [SYN-DROME]

(n) A group of symptoms

SYNTHESIS [SYN-THE-SIS]

(n) The combination of components or elements to form a new whole

SYNTHESIZE [SYN-THE-SIZE]

(n) To make via SYNTHESIS

Also acceptable is SYNTHESISE

Entrepreneur

Sy

SYNTHETIC [SYN-THE-TIC]

(adj) Made to imitate a natural product

SYPHILIS [No F] [SY-PH-ILIS]

(n) A disease

SYRINGE [SY-RIDGE]

(n) A device for sucking and pushing out liquid

SYNONYM [SY-NON-YM]

(n) A word or phrase meaning the same as another word or phrase

T

Ta

TABLE [Ending -LE] [TAB-LE]

(n) A piece of furniture

TACTIC [No K] [TA-C-TIC]

(n) An action with an intended goal

TAE KWON DO [Korean] [TAE K-WON DO]

(n) A type of martial art

TANTALISE [TANT-A-LISE]

(v) To tease with something that is impossible to obtain

Tantalize is US English only

TANTAMOUNT [No D] [TANT-A-MOUNT]

(n) The equivalent

TAPIR [No Y] [TA-PIR]

(v) Piglike herbivorous mammals

TAUNT [TA-U-NT]

Def 1: *(n)* A mocking remark designed to provoke

Def 2: *(v)* To use words to provoke

Te

TECHNIQUE [No K] [TECH-NI-QUE]

(n) A way of doing an activity

TEEPEE [Quadruple E's [TEE-PEE]

(n) A Native American tent

Also acceptable is TEPEE

TELEKINESIS [TELE-KIN-E-SIS]

(n) The power to move objects with the mind

TEMPERATURE [TEMP-ER-A-TURE]

(n) The measure of heat or lack of heat; Unusually high body heat

TENANT [No double N's] [TEN-ANT]

(n) A person who rents a building or property

TENSE [No C] [TEN-SE]

Def 1: *(v)* To make nervous or stressed

Def 2: *(adj)* Nervous and twitchy
To be pulled tight with no slack

Def 3: *(n)* Verbs that indicate time

TENACLE [No I] [Ending -le] [TEN-A-CLE]

(n) A limb with suction cups at the end

TEQUILA [TE-QU-ILA]

(n) A Mexican alcohol spirit

~~terdactal~~ (flying dinosaur) → PTERODACTYL

TERRIBLE [Middle I] [Ending -LE]
[TE-RR-IB-LE]

(n) Awful

TERRIER [Middle I] [Middle double R]
[TE-RR-IER]
(n) A small dog

TESTIMONY [No E] [TEST-I-MONY]

(n) A statement given under oath

TESTOSTERONE [TEST-O-STER-ONE]

(n) The primary male sex hormone

Th

THAW [No F] [T-HAW]

Def 1: *(v)* To unfreeze

Def 2: *(n)* Time of warmer weather warms;
Friendlier relations

~~thawn~~ (baby deer) → FAWN

THEATRE [No U] [Ending -RE] [THE-AT-RE]

(n) A building for plays to be performed;
Related to plays;
A room for operations to be performed

Theater is US English Only

THEFT [THE-FT]

(n) Taken without permission

vs

THIEF [I before E] [THI-EF]

(n) A person who steals

THEIR [THE-IR]

(n) Belong to someone

vs

THERE [THE-RE]

(adv) At a place

THEME [TH-EME]

(n) The subject or style of;
A recuring melody in music

THEMSELVES [No F] [THEM-SELVES]

(pro) A group of people

THEORY [No F] [THE-O-RY]

(n) An unproven explanation

THERAPEUTIC [THER-A-PEU-TIC]

(n) Healing

THERMOSTAT [THER-MO-STAT]

(n) A device to regulate temperature

Th

THESAURUS [THE-SAUR-US]

(n) A book containing synonyms

THESE [No double E] [THE-S-E]

(pl) The plural of THIS

THESIS [THE-SIS]

(n) A theory looking to be agreed upon as being proven

THOROUGH [THO-ROU-GH]

(adj) Complete

THOSE [No double O] [THO-SE]

(pl) Plural of THAT

THOUSAND [THOU-SAND]

(adj) (n) A unit of ten hundreds (1 000)

THOUSANDTH *[No CE]*

THRESHOLD [THRES-HOLD]

(n) A marker indicating the boundary of something

THROUGH [TH-ROU-GH]

(prep) (adv) From one end to another

THREW [Hidden H] [TH-REW]

(v) To throw in the past tense

THRONE [THR-ONE]

(n) The ceremonial seat of a monarch or leader

THROW [Hidden H] [TH-ROW]

(v) To toss through or in the air

THUMB [Hidden H] [TH-UMB]

Def 1: *(n)* A digit on the hand

Def 2: *(v)* To quickly turn pages over;
To gain attention by sticking a thumb up

THUNDER [Hidden H] [THUN-DER]

(n) A loud noise associated with lightning

THWACK [THE-SIS]

Def 1: *(v)* To hit

Def 2: *(n)* A heavy hit

THWART [Hidden H] [TH-WART]

(n) To stop someone's plans

THYME [Hidden H] [TH-YME]

(n) A type of herb

Ti

~~ticoon~~ (business) → TYCOON

time (regarding the herb) → THYME

~~tiphoon~~ (storm) → TYPHOON

~~tirant~~ (oppressor) → TYRANT

TITLE [Ending -LE] [TIT-LE]

> *(n)* The leading name

TISSUE [Double S] [TI-SS-UE]

> *(n)* A disposable handkerchief;
>   What living materials or made of

TITANIC [TIT-AN-IC]

> *(n)* Giant;
> *(proper noun)* A ship that sank after hitting
>   an iceberg on the 15th of April, 1912

TITANIUM [TIT-AN-IUM]

> *(n)* A metallic element

Chemical element symbol = **Ti**
Atomic number = **22**

TOFFEE [Double F] [Double E] [TO-FF-EE]

(n) A type of sweet

TOGETHER [TO-GET-HER]

(adv) In company of

TOILET [TOIL-ET]

(n) A fixed receptacle into which bodily waste may be deposited and hygienically removed

TOMAHAWK [No O] [TOM-A-HAWK]

(n) An axe used by Native Americans

TOMATO [No E] [TO-MAT-TO]

(n) A red fruit (often mistaken for a vegetable) used in salads

TOMB [Silent ending B] [TOM-B]

(n) A monument over a burial place

TOMBSTONE [Silent B] [TOM-B-STONE]

(n) A flat marker for a burial site

To

TOMORROW [Double R] [TO-MOR-ROW]

Def 1: *(adv)* On the day after today

Def 2: *(n)* The day after today

TONGUE [Ending E] [TON-GUE]

(n) An organ in the mouth;
Part of a shoe

TONSIL [TON-SIL]

(n) Two round masses in the back of the throat

TONSILLITIS [Double L] [No U] [TONSIL-LI-TIS]

(n) Inflammation of the tonsils

~~tooshay~~ (acknowledge point) → TOUCHÉ

~~toopay~~ (wig) → TOUPEE

TORAH [Hebrew] [No E] [TOR-AH]

(n) The law of god in Judaism

TORPEDO [One E] [TOR-PE-DO]

(n) An underwater missile

TORQUE [Middle -QU-] [TOR-QUE]

(n) Force causing rotation

TORTOISE [TORT-O-ISE]

(n) A shelled, slow-moving reptile

TOUCHÉ [French] [TOU-CHÉ]

(interjection) Used to appropriateness of an argument or a witty point;
Used to acknowledge a hit in fencing

TOUPEE [TOU-PEE]

(n) A type of wig

TOURNAMENT [No I] [TOURN-A-MENT]

(n) A contest to find the best contender

TOURNIQUET [TOURN-I-QUET]

(n) Cloth tied tightly around an injury to stop blood flow

TOWEL [Ending -LE] [TOW-EL]

(n) A cloth used to dry

Tr

TRAIL [TR-A-IL]

> Def 1: *(n)* A series of signs left to follow;
>   A path

> Def 2: *(v)* To follow

or

TRIAL [TR-I-AL]

> *(n)* An examination of facts;
>   A test of wills

TRAMPOLINE [TRAMP-O-LINE]

> *(n)* An apparatus for bouncing on

TRANSVESTITE [TRANS-VES-TITE]

> *(n)* A person who enjoys dressing as the
>   opposite sex

TRAPEZE [No A] [TRAP-EZE]

> *(n)* A bar for doing acrobatics on

TRAVEL [Single L] [TRAV-EL]

> *(v)* To go from one place to another

TRAVELLER [Double L] [TRAV-ELL-ER]

(n) A person who travels

Traveler is US English Only

TRAVESTY [One R] [TRAV-ESTY]

(n) A shocking injustice

TREACLE [Ending -LE] [TRE-A-CLE]

(n) A thick, sugary liquid

TREK [No C] [TR-EK]

(n) A long walk

TRIAL [TR-I-AL]

(n) An examination of facts;
A test of will

vs

TRAIL [TR-A-IL]

Def 1: *(n)* A series of signs left to follow;
A path

Def 2: *(v)* To follow

Tr

tri (attempt) → TRY

TRIBUTE [TRIB-UTE]
(n) To pay homage to something

TRILLION [TRILL-ION]
(n) A thousand billion (1,000,000,000,000)

TRIUMPH [TRI-UM-PTH]
(n) A success

trist (meeting) → TRYST

TRIVIA [TRI-VIA]
(n) Small bits of information with little value

TRUE [TR-UE]
(n) Correct and accurate

TRULY [No E] (adv)

TRYST [Pronounced TRIST] [TR-YST]
(n) A meeting between lovers

Ts

TSAR [Pronounced *zar*] [T-SAR]

> *(n)* The title of the emperor of Russia

Also acceptable is CZAR

Tu

TUESDAY [Hidden S] [TU-ES-DAY]

> *(n)* The day of the week between Monday and Wednesday

TUXEDO [Pronounced *tux-see-do*] [TUX-E-DO]

> *(n)* Formal evening wear

Ty

TYCOON [TY-COON]

(n) A powers industry person

~~ty kwon do~~ (martial art) → TAE KWON DO

~~tyme~~ (herb) → THYME

TYPHOON [TY-PHOON]

(n) A tropical storm

TYRANNOSAURUS [TY-RAN-NO-SAU-RUS]

(n) A dinosaur species

TYRANT [TY-RANT]

(n) An oppressive person

TYRE [TY-RE]

(n) The rubber covering on a wheel

Tire is US English Only

U

Ub

UBIQUITOUS [U-BI-QUIT-OUS]

(n) Found everywhere;
Commonly associated with

Uc

~~ucalyptus~~ (Australian tree) → EUCALYPTUS

Uh

~~uhponimes~~ (name) → EPONYMOUS

~~uhpostrophe~~ (') → APOSTROPHE

Uk

UKULELE [UK-U-LELE]

> *(n)* A small guitar popularized in Hawaii

Ul

ULTIMATE [ULT-I-MATE]

> *(n)* The best version of

ULTIMATUM [ULTI-MAT-UM]

> *(n)* A final warning to either do something or face the consequences

Um

UMBRELLA [No N] [UM-BRE-LLA]

> *(n)* A folding cover held to avoid the rain or the sun

UMPIRE [No N] [UM-PIRE]

> Def 1: *(n)* A person who referees game
>
> Def 2: *(v)* To umpire

UNCONSCIOUS [UN-CON-SCI-OUS]

(n) Not awake or aware

~~undistinct~~ (unclear) → INDISTINCT

UNINTERESTED [UN-INTER-ESTED]

(adj) Not caring

or

DISINTERESTED [DIS-INTER-ESTED]

(adj) Not biased

UNIQUE [UNI-QUE]

(adj) Being the only one in existence

UNKNOWN [Middle K] [UN-K-NOWN]

(n) Not known or aware of

Up

UPHOLSTERY [UP-HOL-STER-Y]

(n) The padding on soft furniture

Ur

URANIUM [U-RAN-I-UM]

(n) A radioactive element

Chemical element symbol = **U**
Atomic number = **92**

Us

USUAL [US-U-AL]

(adj) Happening regularly

USURP [Not *up*-] [U-SURP]

(v) To take power by force

UTENSIL [UP-HOL-STER-Y]

> *(n)* A tool having a particular use, especially in a kitchen

UTMOST [No P] [UT-MOST]

> *(adj)* Greatest

UVULA [U-V-ULA]

> *(n)* The teardrop shaped flesh hanging at the back of the throat

V

Va

VACCINE [Double C] [No K] [VA-CINE]

(n) A substance used to generate immunity to an infectious disease or pathogen

VACUUM [Double U] [VAC-UU-M]

Def 1: *(n)* A space with nothing in it

Def 2: *(v)* To clean floors

VAGINA [VA-GINA]

(n) Part of a woman's internal genitals serving as the passageway to the womb

VAGUE [VA-G-UE]

(adj) Not conclusive and without detail

VALENTINE [Only one I] [VAL-EN-TINE]

(n) A person you send a card to on February 14th (Valentine's day)

Va

VALET [Pronounced *VAL-AY*] [VAL-ET]

(n) A man's assistance

VALID [VALID]

(n) Acceptable;
Reasonable

VALOUR [VA-LOUR]

(n) Bravery

Valor is US English Only

VALVE [No F] [VA-LVE]

(n) Something that controls flow

VAMPIRE [One P] [VAMP-IRE]

(n) (folklore) A blood sucking monster

VANILLA [Double L] [VAN-ILL-A]

Def 1: *(n)* A flavour

Def 2: *(adj)* Plain

VAPOUR [VAP-OUR]

> *(n)* Moisture suspended in the air

> *Vapor is US English Only*

VARIED [VA-RI-ED]

> *(adj)* Involving different aspects

VAULT [Middle U] [VA-U-LT]

> *(n)* A secure room for storage

Ve

VEGETABLE [VEG-ET-ABLE]

(n) A plant used for food

VEGETARIAN [VEG-ET-AR-IAN]

(n) A person who does not eat meat or fish

VEHICLE [Middle H] [VE-H-ICH-LE]

(n) Something used to transport objects or people

VENEER [VE-NEER]

(n) A thin covering of wood

VERRUCA [Double R] [VER-RU-CA]

(n) A contagious wart on the foot

VERSATILE [VERS-A-TILE]

(adj) Able to be used for many things

VERSION [VER-SION]

(n) Of a similar type but differing in form

~~viacle~~ (Transport) **→ VEHICLE**

VIE [V-IE]

(v) To compete

VIEW [VI-EW]

Def 1: *(n)* The ability to see from a particular position;
An opinion

Def 2: *(v)* To see

VIGIL [No D] [VIG-IL]

(n) A period of paying respects

VIGILANTE [VA-GIL-ANTE]

(n) A person who passes the law to punish people

VIGOUR [VIG-OUR]

(n) Good energy and enthusiasm

Vigor is US English Only

VISCOUNT [Pronounced *VY-COUNT*]
[VIS-COUNT]

(n) A title given by the aristocracy

VISIT [VIS-IT]

(v) To go to

Vo

VOLCANO [VOL-CANO]

> *(n)* A rupture in a planets crust which allows magma to escape from beneath the surface

VOODOO [VOO-DOO]

> *(n)* A religious practise involving spirits

VOWEL [VOW-EL]

> *(n)* A type of letter (A, E, I, O, U)

VOYAGE [VOY-AGE]

> *(n)* A long journey by sea or through space

Vu

~~vurruka~~ (foot wart) → VERRUCA

Vy

~~vycount~~ (title) → VISCOUNT

W

WAFER [One F] [WA-FER]

(n) A thin slice

WAIST [WAI-ST]

(n) The area of the body between the hips and ribs

WALLABY [No E] [WALL-A-BY]

(n) A marsupial from Australia

WARRANTY [Double R] [No E] [WAR-RAN-TY]

(n) A promise to repair or replace something if it breaks

WARMTH [WAR-MTH]

(n) Being warm in nature; Friendly

WARREN [Double R] [WAR-REN]

(n) Interconnected chambers of rabbit burrows

WARRIOR [WAR-RIOR]

(n) A fighter

We

WEAPON [Hidden A] [WEA-PON]

(n) An instrument or device for hurting others

WEATHER [WEA-THER]

Def 1: *(n)* The general state of the atmosphere

Def 2: *(v)* To wear away

or

WETHER [No A] [WE-THER]

(n) A castrated ram

or

WHETHER [No A] [WHE-THER]

(conjunction) A choice

WEAVE [No F] [WEA-VE]

(v) To cross over threads or strands to connect them

WEDNESDAY [Hidden D] [WEN-NES-DAY]

(n) The day after Tuesday and before Thursday

WEIGH [W-EIGH]

(v) To find out how heavy a thing is

vs

WEIGHT [W-EIGHT]

(n) How heavy a thing is

WEIRD [I before E] [W-E-IRD]

(n) Strange

WELD [No A] [W-ELD]

Def 1: *(v)* To join metal together using heat

Def 2: *(n)* A welded joint

WELFARE [One L] [Not -FAIR] [WEL-FARE]

(n) How heavy a thing is

WEREWOLF [WERE-WOLF]

(n) (folklore) A person who turn into a wolf
during a full moon

WETHER [No A] [WE-THER]

(n) A castrated ram

or

WHETHER [No A] [WHE-THER]

(conjunction) A choice

or

WEATHER [WEA-THER]

Def 1: *(n)* The general state of the
atmosphere

Def 2: *(v)* To wear away

WHARF [Hidden H] [WH-A-RF]

> *(n)* A level area for ships to unload and load goods

WHICH [WH-ICH]

> *(adj) (pro)* Asking for more information

or

WITCH [W-IT-CH]

> *(n) (folklore)* A woman that uses magic

WHISPER [Hidden H] [WH-IS-PER]

Def 1: *(v)* To speak softly

Def 2: *(n)* Softley spoken

WHISTLE [Hidden H] [WH-IS-PER]

Def 1: *(n)* A sound made by blowing through the month

Def 2: *(v)* To make a high-pitched noise

Wh

WHITTLE [Double T] [Ending -LE] [WHIT-TLE]

(v) To carve wood

WHOLE [W-HOLE]

Def 1: *(adj)* Complete

Def 2: *(n)* A thing that is complete

or

HOLE [HO-LE]

(n) A hollow in a solid body or surface

WHOSE [One O] [WH-OSE]

(adj) (pro) Belonging to

WIDTH [WID-TH]

> *(n)* The measurement of something from one side another

WIELD [I before e] [WI-ELD]

> *(v)* To control and use a tool or weapon

WIFE [No V] [W-IFE]

> *(adj)* A husbands marriage partner

The plural is WIVES

~~wisper~~ (softly spoken) → WHISPER

WITCH [W-IT-CH]

> *(n) (folklore)* A woman that uses magic

or

WHICH [WH-ICH]

> *(adj) (pro)* Asking for more information

Wi

WILFUL [No double L's] [WIL-FUL]

(adj) Deliberate

Willful is US English Only

WILL-O'-THE-WISP [Three dashes]
[WILL - O' - THE - WISP]

(n) A flame-like light caused by decaying
plant gases in marshy areas;
An elusive goal that misleads

WILLOW [Double L] [WILL-OW]

(n) A type of tree

WITHHOLD [Double H] [WITH-HOLD]

(v) To Suppress

WIVES [No F] [W-IVES]

(n) (pl) The plural of wife

WIZARD [One Z] [WI-Z-ARD]

(n) A man who uses magic

WOEFUL [No double L] [WOE-FUL]

(adj) awful

WOMB [Ending B] [WOM-B]

(n) An organ in female mammals that develops offspring before birth

~~worf~~ (shipping) → WHARF

WOUND [Pronounced *WOO-ND*] [WO-UND]

Def 1: *(v)* To cause injury to

Def 2: *(n)* An injury

is spelt the same as

WOUND [Pronounced *WOW-ND*] [WO-UND]

(v) To wind something in the past

Wr

WREATH [WR-EA-TH]

> *(n)* A circle of picked flowers and leaves

vs

WREATHE [Ending E] [WR-EA-TH-E]

> *(n)* A circle of picked flowers and leaves

~~wright~~ (mark letters) → WRITE

~~wright~~ (correct) → RIGHT

WRITE [WR-ITE]

> *(v)* To mark letters out, either physically or
> digitally

vs

RIGHT [R-IGHT]

Def 1: *(adj)* Morally correct;
> On the east side, opposite to left

Def 2: *(adv)* Correctly

Def 3: *(v)* To correct

Def 4: *(n)* An entitlement

WROUGHT [WRO-UGHT]

(adj) Shaped by hammering

X

If you cannot find the word, first check if it starts with EX- rather than X-

Xe

XENON [Pronounced ZEE-NON] [XE-NON]

(n) A noble gas element

Chemical element symbol = **Xe**
Atomic number = **54**

XENOPHOBIA [XE-NO-PHOBIA]

(n) Fear or dislike of people from other countries

Xy

XYLOPHONE [X-YLO-PHONE]

(n) A musical instrument

Y

Ya

YACHT [Pronounced *YOT*] [YA-CH-T]

>*(n)* A large sailing boat

YAK [No C] [Y-AK]

>*(n)* A large ox with long hair

YARMULKE [Yiddish] [Pronounced *YAR-MUL-KA*] [YAR-MUL-KE]

>*(n)* A Jewish skullcap

Yi

YIELD [Hidden I] [Y-ELD]

>*(v)* To produce;
>To give into demands

Yo

YOGHURT [Hidden H] [YOG-H-URT]

(n) A type of dairy product

YOGURT is also acceptable but is seen as US English

~~yot~~ (sailing boat) → YACHT

~~youbiculouse~~ (common) → UBIQUITOUS

~~youkalaylee~~ (small guitar) → UKULELE

YOUR [YOU-R]

(adj) Belonging to you

vs

YOU'RE [YOU-'-RE]

Contraction of YOU ARE

Yu

YULE [No I] [Y-ULE]

(n) Christmas

Z

Za

ZANY [No S] [Z-A-NY]

(adj) Unconventional

~~zar~~ (Russian Emperor) → TSAR

Ze

ZEBRA [No D] [ZE-BRA]

(n) An African black and white equine

~~zeenon~~ (element) → XENON

~~zeenophobia~~ (prejudice) → XENOPHOBIA

ZEPHYR [Greek] [ZEP-YR]

(n) A light wind

ZEST [Z-EST]

(n) High energy

Zi

ZILCH [Z-ILCH]

(n) (informal) Nothing

ZINC [No K] [Z-INC]

(n) A metallic element

| Chemical element symbol = **Zn** |
| Atomic number = **30** |

Zu

ZUCCHINI [ZU-CC-HI-NI]

(n) An edible squash

Known as COURGETTE in British English

ZWISCHENZUG [German] [ZW-IS-CHEN-ZUG]

(n) An unexpected move that forces the opponent to respond before the expected response is performed, usually found in the context of chess or draughts

ZYGOTE [ZY-GOTE]

(n) Fertilized egg cell that results from the union of a female gamete
(egg, or ovum) with a male gamete (sperm)

Days and Months

Days

Monday	MON-DAY
Tuesday	TU-ES-DAY
Wednesday	WEDNESDAY
Thursday	THUR-S-DAY
Friday	FRI-DAY
Saturday	SAT-UR-DAY
Sunday	SUN-DAY

Months

January	JAN-U-ARY
February	FEB-R-U-ARY
March	MAR-CH
April	AP-RIL
May	MAY
June	JUNE
July	JULY
August	AU-GUST
September	SEP-TEM-BER
October	OCT-O-BER
November	NOV-EM-BER
December	DEC-EM-BER

Sentence Construction

Adjective *(adj)* – A word adding description.

    e.g.: ABYSMAL; BEAUTIFUL; HORRIBLE

Adverb *(adv)* – A word that adds information to a verb, adjective or another adverb.

    e.g.: QUICKLY; RARELY

Auxiliary Verb *(av)* – Minor verbs that help other verbs communicate more complex grammar concepts, like time or existence.

    e.g.: BE; DO; HAVE

Capital *(cap)* – The first letter of a sentence. Names, places and days/months are always capitalised.

Conjunction *(con)* – A word used to connect clauses or sentences.

    e.g.: *FOR; AND; NOR, BUT; OR; YET; SO*

Model Verb *(mv)* – A verb that shows intent, ability, possibility or necessity.

    e.g.: *WILL; CAN; SHOULD; MUST*

Noun *(n)* – A word that represents a person, place, object, thing or concept.

e.g.: MOTHER; TOWN; TULIP; SLIME; CIVILISATION

Preposition *(prep)* – A word before a noun or pronoun that indicates direction, time, space or location.

e.g.: TO ; SINCE; UNDER; AT; FOR

Plural *(pl)* – More than one, usually ending with an S.

e.g.: DOGS; HOUSES

Pronoun *(pro)* – Word(s) that substitute nouns when the person is already known to the subject.

e.g.: YOU; THEY; HE; SHE; WE

Proper Noun *(proper noun)* – A noun that represents a specific person, place, or thing.

e.g.: ANDORRA; HENRY; TITANIC

Verb *(v)* - A word that describe an action, state, or event.

e.g.: RUN; KNOW; BUILT

British English vs US English

British and US English is the same language with variations in spelling and pronunciation.

US English tends to be spelt like it sounds (*phonetically*), unlike British English which stay with the original spelling of the words.

For example, it makes a lot more sense for the word CENTRE to be spelt the US English way (*CENTER*).

But British English retains it's spelling from the original language (in this case old French), meaning it is spelt differently to how it sounds.

The same applies for METRE (*METER*) and LITRE (*LITER*).

In formal writing you should always use the spelling of the area you are in.

British English	US English
Aesthetic	Esthetic
Axe	Ax
Centre	Center
Chequered	Checkered
Colour	Color
Defence	Defense
Disc	Disk
Grey	Gray
Guage	Gage
Labour	Labor
Litre	Liter
Licence	License
Metre	Meter
Moustache	Mustache
Neighbour	Neighbor
Oestrogen	Estrogen
Rumour	Rumor
Theatre	Theater
Tyre	Tire

Countries of the World

Afghanistan	AF-GHAN-I-STAN	*Asia*
Albania	AL-BAN-IA	*Europe*
Algeria	AL-GER-IA	*Africa*
Andorra	AN-DOR-RA	*Europe*
Angola	AN-GO-LA	*Africa*
Antigua and Barbuda	AN-TIG-GUA BAR-BU-DA	*Caribbean*
Argentina	AR-GEN-TINA	*South America*
Armenia	AR-MEN-IA	*Europe*
Australia	AUST-RAL-IA	*Oceania*
Austria	AUST-RIA	*Europe*
Azerbaijan	A-ZER-BAI-JAN	*Asia*

B

Bahamas, The	THE BA-HAM-AS	Caribbean
Bahrain	BA-H-RAIN	Middle East
Bangladesh	BANG-LA-DESH	Asia
Barbados	BAR-BA-DOS	Caribbean
Belarus	BEL-A-RUS	Europe
Belgium	BEL-GI-UM	Europe
Belize	BEL-IZE	North America
Benin	BEN-IN	Africa
Bhutan	B-HUT-AN	Asia
Bolivia	BOL-IV-IA	South America
Bosnia and Herzegovina	BOS-NIA HER-ZE-GOV-INA	Europe
Botswana	BOT-SWAN-A	Africa
Brazil	BRA-ZIL	South America
Brunei	BRU-NEI	Asia
Bulgaria	BUL-GAR-IA	Europe
Burkina Faso	BUR-KINA FASO	Africa
Burundi	BUR-UN-DI	Africa

C

Cabo Verde (Cape Verde)	CABO VERDE	*North America*
Cambodia	CAM-BOD-IA	*Asia*
Cameroon	CAM-E-ROON	*Africa*
Canada	CAN-A-DA	*North America*
Central African Republic	CENT-RAL AF-RI-CAN RE-PUBLIC	*Africa*
Chad	CHAD	*Africa*
Chile	CH-ILE	*South America*
China	C-HINA	*Asia*
Colombia	CO-LOM-BIA	*South America*
Comoros	COM-OR-OS	*Africa*
Costa Rica	COSTA RICA	*North America*
Côte d'Ivoire (Ivory Coast)	CÔTE D'IVO-IRE	*Africa*
Croatia	CRO-A-TIA	*Europe*
Cuba	CUBA	*Caribbean*
Cyprus	CY-P-RUS	*Europe*
Czechia (Czech Republic)	CZE-CHIA	*Europe*

D

Democratic Republic of the Congo	DEMO-CRATIC RE-PUBLIC OF THE CONGO	*Africa*
Denmark	DEN-MARK	*Europe*
Djibouti	D-JI-BOU-TI	*Europe*
Dominica	DO-MIN-I-CA	*Caribbean*
Dominican Republic	DOM-IN-I-CAN RE-PUBLIC	*Caribbean*

E

East Timor *(Timor-Leste)*	EAST TIMOR	*Asia*
Ecuador	E-CU-A-DOR	*South America*
Egypt	EG-Y-PT	*Africa*
El Salvador	EL SAL-VA-DOR	*North America*
England *[Part of the UK]*	EN-G-LAND	*Europe*
Equatorial Guinea	EQUATOR-IAL GU-IN-EA	*Africa*
Eritrea	ER-IT-REA	*Africa*
Estonia	EST-ONIA	*Europe*
Eswatini *(Swaziland)*	E-SWAN-TI-NI	*Africa*
Ethiopia	ETH-IO-PIA	*Africa*

F

Fiji	FI-JI	*Oceania*
Finland	FIN-LAND	*Europe*
France	FRAN-CE	*Europe*

G

Gabon	GA-BON	*Africa*
Gambia, The	THE GAM-BIA	*Africa*
Georgia	GEORGIA	*Europe*
Germany	GER-MANY	*Europe*
Ghana	GH-ANA	*Africa*
Greece	GR-EE-CE	*Europe*
Grenada	GRE-ADA	*Caribbean*
Guatemala	GUAT-E-MALA	*North America*
Guinea	GU-IN-EA	*Africa*
Guinea-Bissau	GUINEA-BISSAU	*Europe*
Guyana	GUY-ANA	*South America*

H

Haiti	HAI-TI	*Caribbean*
Honduras	HON-DU-RAS	*South America*
Hungary	HUNG-ARY	*Europe*

I

Iceland	ICE-LAND	*Europe*
India	IN-DIA	*Asia*
Indonesia	IN-DON-ESIA	*Asia*
Iran	IRAN	*Middle East*
Iraq	IRAQ	*Middle East*
Ireland	IRE-LAND	*Europe*
Israel	IS-RA-EL	*Middle East*
Italy	ITALY	*Europe*

J

Jamaica	JAM-A-I-CA	*Caribbean*
Japan	JAPAN	*Asia*
Jordan	JOR-DAN	*Middle East*

K

Kazakhstan	KAZ-AK-H-STAN	*Asia*
Kenya	KEN-YA	*Africa*
Kiribati	KIR-I-BATI	*Oceania*
Kosovo	KOS-O-VO	*Europe*
Kuwait	KU-WAIT	*Middle East*
Kyrgyzstan	KY-RG-YZ-STAN	*Asia*

L

Laos	LAOS	*Asia*
Latvia	LAT-VIA	*Europe*
Lebanon	LEB-ANON	*Middle East*
Lesotho	LES-O-THO	*Africa*
Liberia	LI-BER-IA	*Africa*
Libya	LIB-YA	*Africa*
Liechtenstein	LIE-CH-TEN-STEIN	*Europe*
Lithuania	LIT-HUAN-IA	*Europe*
Luxembourg	LUX-EM-BOURG	*Europe*

M

Madagascar	MAD-A-GAS-CAR	*Africa*
Malawi	MAL-A-WI	*Africa*
Malaysia	MAL-AY-SIA	*Asia*
Maldives	MAL-DIVES	*Asia*
Mali	MALI	*Africa*
Malta	MAL-TA	*Europe*
Marshall Islands	MARSHALL IS-LANDS	*Oceania*
Mauritania	MAUR-IT-AN-IA	*Africa*
Mauritius	MAUR-IT-IUS	*Africa*
Mexico	MEX-I-CO	*North America*
Micronesia, Federated States of	MICRO-NESIA	*Oceania*
Moldova	MOL-DO-VA	*Europe*
Monaco	MON-A-CO	*Europe*
Mongolia	MON-GOL-IA	*Asia*
Montenegro	MON-TE-NE-GRO	*Europe*
Morocco	MOR-O-CC-O	*Africa*
Mozambique	MOZ-AM-BI-QUE	*Africa*
Myanmar (Burma)	MY-AN-MAR	*Asia*

N

Namibia	NAM-I-BIA	*Africa*
Nauru	NA-UR-U	*Oceania*
Nepal	NE-PAL	*Asia*
Netherlands	NETHER-LANDS	*Europe*
New Zealand	NEW ZEA-LAND	*Oceania*
Nicaragua	NIC-ARA-GUA	*North America*
Niger	NI-GER	*Africa*
Nigeria	NI-GER-IA	*Africa*
North Korea	NORTH KO-REA	*Asia*
North Macedonia	NORTH MACE-DO-NIA	*Europe*
Northern Ireland *[Part of the UK]*	NORTH-ERN IRELAND	*Europe*
Norway	NOR-WAY	*Europe*

O

Oman	OMAN	*Middle East*

P

Pakistan	PAK-I-STAN	*Asia*
Palau	PAL-AU	*Oceania*
Palestine*	PAL-E-STIN-E	*Middle East*
Panama	PAN-A-MA	*North America*
Papua New Guinea	PAP-UA NEW GU-IN-EA	*Asia*
Paraguay	PARA-G-UAY	*South America*
Peru	PERU	*South America*
Philippines	PHILIP-PINES	*Africa*
Poland	PO-LAND	*Europe*
Portugal	PORT-U-GAL	*Europe*

*Disputed: Internationally considered part of Israel but Palestine maintains its own sovereignty

Q

QATAR	Q-AT-AR	*Middle East*

R

Republic of the Congo	RE-PUBLIC OF THE CONGO	*Africa*
Romania	RO-MAIN-IA	*Europe*
Russia	RU-SS-IA	*Europe/ Asia*
Rwanda	R-W-AN-DA	*Africa*

S

Saint Kitts and Nevis	SAINT KITTS NEVIS	*Caribbean*
Saint Lucia	SAINT LUC-IA	*Caribbean*
Saint Vincent and the Grenadines	SAINT VINCENT GREN-A-DINES	*Caribbean*
Samoa	SA-MO-A	*Oceania*
San Marino	SAN MAR-INO	*Europe*
Sao Tome and Principe	SAO TOME PRINCIPE	*North America*
Saudi Arabia	SAUDI AR-A-BIA	*Middle East*
Scotland [Part of the UK]	SCOT-LAND	*Europe*
Senegal	SEN-E-GAL	*Africa*
Serbia	SER-BIA	*Europe*
Seychelles	SEY-CELL-ES	*Africa*
Sierra Leone	SI-ERRA LE-ONE	*Africa*
Singapore	SING-A-PORE	*Asia*
Slovakia	SLO-VA-KIA	*Europe*
Slovenia	SLO-VEN-IA	*Europe*

S

Solomon Islands	SOLOMON ISLANDS	*Oceania*
Somalia	SOM-A-LIA	*Africa*
South Africa	SOUTH AFRICA	*Africa*
South Sudan	SOUTH SUDAN	*Africa*
South Korea	SOUTH KO-REA	*Asia*
Spain	SPAIN	*Europe*
Sri Lanka	SRI LAN-KA	*Asia*
Sudan	SUDAN	*Africa*
Suriname	SUR-I-NAME	*South America*
Sweden	SWE-DEN	*Europe*
Switzerland	SWIT-ZER-LAND	*Europe*

T

Taiwan *	TAI-WAN	*Asia*
Tajikistan	TA-JIKI-STAN	*Asia*
Tanzania	TAN-ZAN-IA	*Asia*
Thailand	THAI-LAND	*Asia*
Togo	TOGO	*Africa*
Tonga	TON-GA	*Oceania*
Trinidad and Tobago	TRIN-I-DAD TO-BA-GO	*Caribbean*
Tunisia	TU-NIS-IA	*Africa*
Türkiye (Turkey)	TÜRK-I-YE	*Asia*
Turkmenistan	TURK-MEN-I-STAN	*Asia*
Tuvalu	TU-VA-LU	*Oceania*

*Disputed: Internationally considered part of China but Taiwan maintains its own sovereignty

U

Uganda	U-GAN-DA	*Africa*
Ukraine	UK-RAIN-E	*Europe*
United Arab Emirates	UNITED ARAB EMIR-ATES	*Middle East*
United Kingdom (UK)	UNITED KINGDOM	*Europe*
United States	UNITED STATES	*North America*
Uruguay	UR-A-GUAY	*South America*
Uzbekistan	UZ-BEK-I-STAN	*Asia*

V

Vanuatu	VAN-U-A-TU	*Oceania*
Vatican City	VAT-I-CAN CITY	*Europe*
Venezuela	VEN-E-ZU-ELA	*South America*
Vietnam	VEIT-NAM	*Asia*

W

Wales [Part of the UK]	WA-LES	*Europe*

Y

Yemen	YE-MEN	*Middle East*

Z

Zambia	ZAM-BIA	*Africa*
Zimbabwe	ZIM-BAB-WE	*Africa*